VOYAGES
IN ENGLISH

Writing and Grammar

Grade 8 Practice Book

Elaine de Chantal Brookes

Patricia Healey

Irene Kervick

Catherine Irene Masino

Anne B. McGuire

Adrienne Saybolt

LOYOLAPRESS.

ISBN: 0-8294-2097-5

LOYOLAPRESS.

3441 N. ASHLAND AVENUE
CHICAGO, ILLINOIS 60657
(800) 621-1008
www.LoyolaPress.org

05 06 07 08 09 10 11 12 13 14 VH 10 9 8 7 6 5 4 3 2 1

CONTENTS

CHAPTER 1

Singular and Plural Nouns

● **Underline the singular noun in each sentence. Then write the plural form of the noun. Use a dictionary if necessary.**

1. She was sworn in after reciting an oath. _____

2. The moose ran faster than I imagined it could. _____

3. I like studying at the library. _____

4. The woman next door is kind and generous. _____

5. I noticed that one antenna was missing. _____

6. He saw a mouse scampering between the boxes. _____

7. The caravan stopped at an oasis. _____

8. Each hoof needed to be cleaned. _____

9. I watched as the huge bear slept. _____

10. Did you see that beautiful red fox? _____

11. She showed us the delicate antique tray. _____

CHAPTER 1

More Singular and Plural Nouns

● **Underline the singular noun in each sentence. Then go back and circle the first letter of each plural noun. Write the letters in order on the lines below to find the answer to the riddle.**

1. Ten monkeys swung from the vine.

2. I heard faint echoes coming from the cave.

3. We are alumni of the same school.

4. The shelves in the kitchen need to be rearranged.

5. He rides unicycles in the circus.

6. She uses home remedies to treat a cold.

7. How many exits are in this building?

8. Five moose stepped into the clearing.

9. He has three eights in his card hand.

10. How many nuclei are in a single cell?

11. Grace caught six trout.

What is an inchworm's favorite math skill?
Answer: ___ ___ ___ ___ ___ ___ ___ ___ ___ ___ ___
        1   2   3   4   5   6   7   8   9 10 11

Now use your answer in a sentence.

_____

CHAPTER 1
What Makes a Good Personal Narrative?

● **Read the personal narrative. Then answer the questions.**

> I could hardly believe it. Every step and every move was perfect! I had spent six long months learning the routine. It seemed every time I performed the dance in rehearsal, I had made a mistake. Once I forgot my dance shoes. But this time, with the spotlight shining brightly on me, blinding my eyes to the audience and tingling my skin, I felt myself dancing as if I were in a dream. The music flowed through my veins like blood, the pounding of the drums keeping time with the pounding of my heart. I wasn't just dancing to the music, I was the music.

1. What would be the best title for this personal narrative—"Dance Rehearsal" or "Dancing a Dream?"

   _____

   Why do you think so?

   _____

2. Who do you think is the intended audience for this narrative? Why do you think so?

   _____

3. What reaction do you think the author wants from the reader? What kind of feelings and emotions is he or she trying to invoke?

   _____

4. The author included one irrelevant detail. What is it?

   _____

5. This narrative is told in chronological order. What words did the author use to provide coherence?

   _____

   _____

CHAPTER 1
Nouns as Subjects and Subject Complements

● Circle the letter under *Subject* if the underlined noun is the subject of the sentence. Circle the letter under *Complement* if the underlined noun renames the subject. Write the circled letters in order on the lines below. If your answers are correct, the answer to the riddle will be revealed.

	Subject	Complement
1. Ms. Hernandez is our new science <u>teacher</u>.	A	S
2. <u>Jesse</u> bought a new jacket with his allowance.	W	O
3. The <u>sun</u> is rising over the mountain.	I	R
4. Jazzy was my mom's big tiger-striped <u>cat</u>.	E	N
5. The white <u>rabbit</u> scrambled under the fence.	E	T
6. Lisa's <u>bicycle</u> got a flat tire on the way to school.	W	L
7. Gina and Chantel were the most talented <u>dancers</u> I knew.	A	H
8. She became my <u>friend</u> at summer camp.	O	I
9. My <u>brother</u> used to play professional tennis.	N	M
10. Maya remained the <u>president</u> of the computer company.	H	E

What do you call a pig's complaint?

Answer: ___ ___ ___ ___ ___ ___ ___ ___ ___ ___
 1   2   3   4   5   6   7   8   9 10

CHAPTER 1

Nouns as Objects and Object Complements

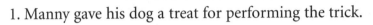

● **Circle the noun used as an indirect object in each sentence. Count the letters in each answer and write the number in the box.**

1. Manny gave his dog a treat for performing the trick.

2. The community center offers people a variety of classes.

3. Jon sent Maria an invitation to the winter dance.

4. Did Krista give the aerialist the award?

5. The postal worker brought the manager a package.

● **Circle the term used as an object complement in each sentence. Count the letters in each answer and write the number in the box.**

6. We named our new pet snake Bowe.

7. Kyra decided to appoint Elena club secretary.

8. Sergio and Jake considered the coaches their friends.

9. The girls chose Cherise "Miss Congeniality."

10. The critics called the new show a disaster.

● **Now crack the code. Use the key below to write the letter for each number on the lines below. If your answers are correct, you'll answer the riddle.**

Who always hurries but is never late?

3 = J   4 = N   5 = S   6 = U   7 = I   8 = E   9 = T   16 = M

Answer: ___ ___ ___ ___ ___ ___   ___ ___ ___ ___
        3   6   5   9   7   4   9   7   16   8

CHAPTER 1

Introduction, Body, and Conclusion

- **A personal narrative includes an introduction, a body, and a conclusion. Write *I, B,* or *C* to show whether each of the following sentences would most likely come in the introduction, body, or conclusion of a personal narrative.**

1. _____ I sat back and closed my eyes; it was finally over.

2. _____ Little did I know that I would never again return to Thor Mountain.

3. _____ When I woke up that morning, it seemed like any other day.

4. _____ We ran as fast as we could as the bear followed close behind.

5. _____ The wind howled like a wild animal outside my window.

6. _____ I don't like to tell secrets, but this one was too good to keep to myself!

- **Choose a personal narrative topic from the list. Write an engaging introduction for a personal narrative about the topic.**

winning a championship game	death of a grandparent
a summer adventure	moving to another city
finding a lost pet	

_____

_____

_____

- **Plan the rest of your narrative by completing a Word/Idea Web like the one on page 137. Draw your web on a separate sheet of paper.**

© Loyola Press

Appositives

CHAPTER 1

● **Circle each noun used as an appositive and underline the noun it explains.**

1. Corey, my little brother, is the noisiest person I've ever met.

2. Jill loves potatoes, the tastiest vegetable in the world—or so she claims.

3. We should contact Mr. Sanchez, Miguel's coach, for a meeting.

4. Wendy traveled to London, the capital of England, to visit her pen pal.

5. The penguin, a flightless bird, lives near the South Pole.

6. My sister, Maggie, makes the best cookies.

7. Dr. Fredricks, a college professor, will speak to our class tomorrow.

8. The novel *Holes* won a Newbery Medal.

● **Write four sentences that use a noun as an appositive.**

9. _____

_____

10. _____

_____

11. _____

_____

12. _____

_____

Possessive Nouns

● **Rewrite each sentence so that the appropriate noun shows possession. The first one is done for you.**

1. The reports written by Min and Juvia were excellent.

   Min's and Juvia's reports were excellent.

2. The father of McKenzie and Trent is a famous writer.

   _____

3. The tree house belonging to the boys is over the stream.

   _____

4. The most familiar story written by Charles Dickens is about a boy named Pip.

   _____

5. These old books belonging to my father-in-law are priceless.

   _____

6. Tham borrowed the bike owned by her best friend.

   _____

7. The toys belonging to the children were scattered across the floor.

   _____

8. The pie made by Ben and Theo won first prize at the fair.

   _____

9. The purse belonging to that woman was stolen at the park.

   _____

10. Manners should be the priority of every gentleman.

   _____

CHAPTER 1

Time Lines

● **Create a narrative paragraph using the time line below. Use transition words and phrases to make the events flow together logically.**

A Hiking Disaster

10:00 a.m.   went hiking in the mountains with my best friend

12:00 p.m.   sat down by stream for lunch
                   friend dropped map in stream; it floated away

1:00 p.m.   couldn't find trail; wandered

9:00 p.m.   ducked under rocks
                   fell asleep

5:00 a.m.   awakened by barks
                   saved by rescue dogs

_____
_____
_____
_____
_____
_____
_____
_____

CHAPTER 1

Descriptive Adjectives and Position of Adjectives

- **Complete each sentence with the most appropriate descriptive adjectives from the box. Use each word only once.**

difficult	fragrant	fragile	ferocious	spicy
talented	unfair	soggy	antique	colorful
shiny	sunny	fluffy	delicious	blue
nervous	humorous	delighted	frightened	painful

1. The _____ lion growled at the _____ hunters.

2. _____ clouds powdered the _____ summer sky.

3. Charla's _____ reading chair is quite _____.

4. Please help me hang these _____ clothes in the _____ backyard.

5. The _____ clown made the children _____.

6. Mom's homemade pizza was _____ but _____.

7. This _____ social studies test makes me _____.

8. Tessa's horse is so _____ that it has won many _____ trophies.

9. Grandma's flower garden is _____ and _____.

10. Oh no, that judge's ruling is extremely _____!

- **Now go back and write *D* (for a regular *descriptive adjective*), *SC* (for a descriptive adjective used as a *subject complement*), or *OC* (for a descriptive adjective used as an *object complement*) above each of the adjectives you wrote.**

(Hint: The usual position of a descriptive adjective is *before* the noun it describes. A descriptive adjective used as a subject complement or as an object complement often comes *after* the verb or direct object.)

CHAPTER 1

Demonstrative, Interrogative, and Indefinite Adjectives

● **Underline the demonstrative or interrogative adjective in each sentence. Write *D* if the adjective is demonstrative and *I* if it is interrogative.**

1. Those flowers belong to my sister. _____

2. Which backpack is yours? _____

3. What name did you give the puppy? _____

4. That painting took me four days to complete. _____

5. Which road did you decide to take? _____

6. He asked, "What museums do you want to visit?" _____

7. Did you wear this dress for the wedding? _____

8. These boys won't let us play baseball with them. _____

9. Which video game do you want to buy? _____

10. I found the stray kittens in this garage. _____

● **Complete each sentence with an indefinite adjective from the box. Use each word only once. Then go back to check whether any other words from the box would also fit. Write that word on the line after the sentence. If no other word fits, write *NO*.**

any	all	another	both	few
many	much	several	some	such

11. _____ vegetables are tastier than others. _____

12. There are _____ shoes to choose from. _____

13. How _____ money did you bring? _____

14. I did not see _____ deer in the woods that day. _____

15. Here is _____ test for you to grade. _____

16. There are too _____ students in the class. _____

17. May I have a _____ coins for the meter? _____

18. I like to taste _____ chocolate. _____

CHAPTER 1

Varied Sentences

- **Identify each type of sentence by circling *S* (simple), *CD* (compound), or *CX* (complex). Then, for each compound or complex sentence you find, separate it into the two or more sentences that were combined. Write these simple sentences on the lines, adding or deleting words as needed.**

1. Lin wanted spaghetti for dinner, but Tom wanted hamburgers.　　S　CD　CX

_____

_____

2. Baseball, soccer, and tennis are Terrance's favorite sports.　　S　CD　CX

_____

_____

3. Brandon, Joe's little brother, was the funniest person in the class.　　S　CD　CX

_____

_____

4. The cat ran under the fence, and the dog followed in hot pursuit.　　S　CD　CX

_____

_____

5. Jessica loves visiting her cousins because they live on a big farm.　　S　CD　CX

_____

_____

6. Though he is behind in his math homework, Bryan is ahead in English.　　S　CD　CX

_____

_____

CHAPTER 1

Comparative and Superlative Adjectives

- **Read each sentence. Check to see if the comparative or superlative adjective is used correctly. If it is used correctly, write *C* on the line. If it is not used correctly, write the correct comparative or superlative adjective on the line.**

1. Theresa's hair is *much longer* than Sara's.   _____

2. Emilio is the *more smarter* person in my class.   _____

3. My aunt is the *most intelligent* woman I know.   _____

4. Carrie shared her *deepest* secrets with me.   _____

5. The cheetah is one of the *most fastest* animals on earth.   _____

6. Casanova is *prettier* than my other cats.   _____

7. Is that the *highest* mountain you've ever climbed?   _____

8. Jenny's eyes are *darkest* than mine.   _____

9. Shane is *more taller* than Jared this year.   _____

10. Mr. Grant was the *more interesting* speaker of them all. _____

- **Now go back and read each sentence again. Circle the noun each adjective modifies.**

- **Write three of your own sentences, comparing these nouns:**
  A. two foods
  B. three friends
  C. two sports

  A. _____

  _____

  B. _____

  _____

  C. _____

  _____

CHAPTER 1

Few and *Little* with Count and Noncount Nouns

- **Write the correct adjective—*few, fewer, fewest, little, less,* or *least*—to complete each sentence. Circle the letter under *Count* if the adjective modifies a count noun. Circle the letter under *Noncount* if the adjective modifies a noncount noun.**

	Count	Noncount
1. There is _____ corn on his plate than mine.	W	S
2. Justin had the _____ money of anyone in the group.	I	T
3. We coached _____ players this year than last.	E	R
4. There are only a _____ minutes left in the hour.	P	C
5. Make sure to give this puppy a _____ love every day.	A	O
6. We have only a _____ books on the shelves in the corner.	N	M
7. My garden produced _____ flowers than expected.	N	U
8. Will you put a _____ mustard on my hot dog?	H	O
9. Nathan has constructed the _____ model cars.	P	L
10. There are _____ brownies left at the bake sale.	E	A
11. Of all subjects, I have the _____ knowledge in biology.	R	T
12. There is _____ peace left in that part of the world.	E	S

- **Now go back and circle three abstract nouns.**

- **Read the circled letters in order, from top to bottom and bottom to top. Then write the letters on the lines below.**

Answer: ___ ___ ___ ___   ___ ___   ___ ___   ___ ___ ___ ___
          1   2   3   4   5   6   7   8   9 10 11 12

What do you notice about these letters?

_____

CHAPTER 1

Exact Words

- **Write specific, interesting adjectives, verbs, or adverbs to complete each sentence. Avoid overused words such as *big, very, nice, pretty, good, great,* and *bad*.**

1. We _____ over the _____ bridge before the hunters could catch us.

2. Josh became _____ impatient with his _____ little brother Jake.

3. Bring in the horses before that _____ fire can _____ the wheat field!

4. Tara giggled _____ as all eyes _____ at her, waiting for her speech.

- **The verb *said* is one of the most overused words in the English language. Underline the word used in place of *said* in each sentence. Then find and circle these six words in the word search below. Words can go across, up, down, and diagonal.**

"I just don't know," Mom sighed.   Lisa shouted, "Don't open that door!"

"How are you?" Jason inquired shyly.   "Please bring in the trash," Dad pleaded.

"That painting is beautiful," he whispered.   "That is hilarious!" she laughed.

```
S  X  G  L  W  G  B  C  M  L  I  O  G  N
A  I  W  D  F  H  G  J  K  A  L  M  O  E
Z  N  N  H  S  K  I  V  C  U  M  N  L  D
S  Q  A  I  O  U  D  S  L  G  A  B  E  E
V  U  F  B  C  P  U  T  P  H  F  G  E  T
S  I  G  H  E  D  G  E  Y  E  T  R  S  U
O  R  E  P  L  E  A  D  E  D  R  G  N  O
P  E  M  K  L  K  S  X  E  C  V  E  M  H
N  D  Y  E  H  I  J  H  G  M  B  I  D  S
```

CHAPTER 1

Adjective Phrases and Clauses

● Draw a line from each subject in the first column to the item in the second column that creates the best complete sentence. Then underline each adjective phrase or clause. Write *AP* on the line if it is an adjective phrase and *AC* if it is an adjective clause.

_____	1. The tiger	on freeways drive too fast.
_____	2. The cruise ship,	who is willing to practice may make the pros.
_____	3. Rivers	in the brush has golden eyes.
_____	4. The girl	which is in the harbor, is going to Mexico.
_____	5. Some people	who never learn to apologize.
_____	6. Parrots	with the button eyes is old and worn.
_____	7. Italy	that provide drinking water are plentiful.
_____	8. An athlete	is a country with many famous tourist attractions.
_____	9. The teddy bear	with red hair gave me a valentine.
_____	10. Sorry are those	that can learn to talk cost a lot of money.

Voyages in English 8

CHAPTER 1

Self-Assessment

● Check *Always*, *Sometimes*, or *Never* to respond to each statement.

Writing	Always	Sometimes	Never
I can identify a personal narrative and its features.			
I understand how to write an effective introduction, body, and conclusion for a personal narrative.			
I can use a time line to organize my ideas.			
I use a variety of sentences (simple, compound, and complex) in my writing.			
I use specific, interesting words in my writing.			
I include all the key features in a personal narrative.			

Grammar	Always	Sometimes	Never
I can identify and use singular and plural nouns.			
I can identify and use nouns as subjects and subject complements.			
I can identify and use nouns as objects and object complements.			
I can identify and use appositives.			
I can identify nouns used to show singular and plural possession and use them correctly.			
I can identify nouns used to show joint possession and use them correctly.			
I can identify and use descriptive adjectives and determine when they are used as subject complements and object complements.			
I can identify and use demonstrative, interrogative, and indefinite adjectives.			
I can identify and use comparative and superlative adjectives.			
I can identify and use *few* and *little* with count and noncount nouns.			
I can identify and use adjective phrases and adjective clauses.			

● **What was the most helpful thing you learned in this chapter?**

_____

_____

Person, Number, and Gender of Pronouns

● Underline the pronoun in each sentence. Write the pronoun's person (*first, second, third*) and number (*singular, plural*). Then identify the gender (*masculine, feminine, neuter*) of all <u>third person singular pronouns</u> or place an *X* when gender doesn't apply. The first one is done for you.

	Person	Number	Gender
1. Mina and <u>I</u> shared an ice-cream sundae.	first	singular	X
2. Josh, did you call last night?			
3. The lawn mower belongs to them.			
4. Kylie handed him the first-place trophy.			
5. The house we want to buy is far away.			
6. She is Katie's best friend.			
7. The dog was thirsty, so Vinh gave it water.			
8. Does the teacher have tickets for us?			
9. They will bring potato salad to the picnic.			
10. Jack gave her a kitten for Christmas.			

CHAPTER

2

Subject Pronouns

● **Circle the subject pronoun that correctly completes each sentence.**

1. The ones who won first place were Mia and (I   me).

2. Jerri and (she   her) are the only ones who like peas.

3. It was (we   us) who brought the chocolate cake.

4. The lionesses lying under the tree are Sheba and (her   she).

5. (Them   They) are both successful lawyers.

6. (Him   He) and Booker both hit home runs in the game.

7. Did (it   you) know that cats walk on their toes?

8. Theo, did (you   your) remember to lock the door?

9. Darius is talented, but (him   he) still needs lots of practice.

10. The people who moved in next door were (they   them).

● **Now go back and underline the first letter of each answer. Use the key below to decode the letters you underlined. Write the letters, in order to fill in the boxes. If your answers are correct, you will have a palindrome (a word or sentence that reads the same forward and backward) that answers this question:**

What is zero, no matter what?

| I = N | T = R | H = O | W = V | S = E | Y = D |

1.	2.	3.	4.	5.	6.	7.	8.

9.	10.		E	V	E	N

CHAPTER
2

What Makes a Good How-to Article?

● **A good how-to article includes concise, logically ordered steps. Read the how-to paragraph. Delete three unnecessary or illogical sentences. Then circle six transition words that help the reader know the order of the steps.**

Fluffy, Shake!

Most people think a cat cannot be trained, but they are wrong. Cats are intelligent creatures that are highly responsive to suggestion, just as dogs are. Most people are cat lovers. First, decide on a behavior that you'd like your cat to learn, such as shaking your hand. Dogs are also easily trained. Second, make sure you have plenty of treats ready to reinforce your cat's behavior. Begin by placing the treat in the center of your hand where your cat can't see it. Next, reach down and wait for your cat to reach for the food with its paw. Then, as your cat reaches up, say firmly, "Shake." Give your cat the treat if it performs correctly. You want your cat to associate your extended hand and the word *shake* with a tasty treat. You can find cat treats and toys in your local pet store. Repeat this step several times. Finally, try it without the treat. Your cat should reach up to see if there is something tasty in your hand. Keep practicing, and believe it or not, you can train your cat!

● **Answer the following questions about this how-to paragraph.**

1. Who would be the best audience for this how-to paragraph? Why?

_____

2. What is the first step in training your cat to perform a trick?

_____

What is the last step?

_____

3. What is the conclusion of this paragraph? What does it promise or predict?

_____

4. Write another introductory sentence for this paragraph. Remember that the introduction should grab the reader's attention and tell what the paragraph is about.

_____

CHAPTER 2

Object Pronouns

● Underline the object pronoun in each sentence. Then tell how the pronoun is used by crossing out the letter in the corresponding column.

	Direct Object	Indirect Object	Object of a Prep.
1. The next class production was chosen by Leah and me.	G	O	R
2. We chose Shakespeare, who gave us beautiful words.	O	T	D
3. I've heard many fascinating stories about him.	G	R	I
4. Thirty-seven full-length plays were written by him.	A	M	H
5. The theater-going crowds of England loved him.	S	M	A
6. Shakespeare wrote plays about love, history, and tragedy for them.	R	M	E
7. Shakespeare was married to Anne Hathaway, but he did not take her to London.	O	E	A
8. Queen Elizabeth supported the arts, and Shakespeare performed for her several times.	N	S	E
9. His theater, the Globe, was closed in 1642, but art patrons rebuilt it in 1995.	W	G	O
10. Shakespeare liked to entertain people, and he delighted them with puns and comic characters.	L	O	D

● Now write the leftover letters in order from left to right on the lines below to spell out a sentence.

Answer: ___ ___ ___ ___ ___ ___ ___ ___ ___ ___ ___
        1 1 2 2   3 3 4 4 5 5 6

___ ___ ___ ___ ___ ___ ___ ___ ___ g r a d e s .
 6 7 7 8 8   9 9 10 10

CHAPTER
2

Pronouns after *Than* or *As*

● Replace the underlined word or words with the correct pronoun
in each sentence. Then write any words that are missing but
understood. The first one is done for you.

	Prounoun	Missing Words
1. Troy is much more athletic than <u>Michael</u>.	he	is athletic
2. Those students performed as well as <u>these students</u>.		
3. Our baseball team won more games than <u>the Tigers</u>.		
4. I like chocolate cake more than <u>Jerome</u>.		
5. Marcus ran no farther than <u>our team</u>.		
6. Jordan plays racquetball as well as <u>Lauren</u>.		
7. I'm sure that I can dance as well as <u>Ms. Thompson</u>.		
8. The fifth-hour class thinks that it will raise more money than <u>our class</u>.		

● Write the four letters that appear in the pronouns you wrote to spell
a direction.

Answer: ___ ___ ___ ___

● Now use those four letters to solve this riddle with two nearly
rhyming words.

What do you call loving bird sounds?

Answer: ___ ___ ___ ___ ___   ___ ___ ___ ___ ___ ___

CHAPTER 2

Making Instructions Clear and Concise

- **One way to make instructions clear and concise is to have good organization. The steps should come in chronological order (1–9). Number in the correct order these steps for making French toast.**

A. ☐ Place bread slices in the hot pan or on the griddle.

B. ☐ Turn over the bread in the mixture so that both sides are coated.

C. ☐ Cover your French toast with butter, syrup, powdered sugar, fresh berries, whipped cream, or other toppings of your choice. Eat!

D. ☐ In a bowl beat together two eggs, 1/4 tsp. vanilla, 1/8 cup milk, and a dash of salt.

E. ☐ When the second side is done, place the toast on a serving plate.

F. ☐ Gather the ingredients.

G. ☐ Let butter melt in a large frying pan or on a griddle while you mix the ingredients.

H. ☐ Place the bread in the egg mixture.

I. ☐ Flip bread over after the first side is golden brown.

- **On a separate piece of paper, list the steps for making one of your favorite dishes. Number your steps in chronological order.**

CHAPTER 2

Possessive Pronouns and Adjectives

● **Rewrite each sentence with a correct possessive pronoun or adjective.**

1. Our has lemon trees.

   _____

2. I think that backpack is your's.

   _____

3. My is the best of the bunch.

   _____

4. Her will crack if you are not careful.

   _____

5. There snow blower broke yesterday.

   _____

6. My requires extra maintenance.

   _____

7. His' painting was too beautiful to describe.

   _____

8. Hours is painted yellow.

   _____

9. His's seems sluggish.

   _____

10. They'res are floating on the pond.

    _____

● **Use the following possessive pronoun in an original sentence.**

11. mine

    _____

CHAPTER 2

Intensive and Reflexive Pronouns

● **Complete each sentence with the correct intensive or reflexive pronoun. Identify each pronoun by circling *I* for intensive or *R* for reflexive.**

	Intensive	Reflexive
1. You may all find _____ lost without a map.	I	R
2. Maria must give _____ time to study.	I	R
3. I _____ am unable to attend the wedding.	I	R
4. You can teach the class _____.	I	R
5. He _____ ran the marathon.	I	R
6. We allowed _____ to enjoy the scenery.	I	R
7. They will plant new trees _____.	I	R
8. The horse _____ could win the race.	I	R

● **Use each pronoun in a sentence.**

9. itself _____

10. themselves _____

11. yourself _____

12. herself _____

13. ourselves _____

14. himself _____

CHAPTER

2 Revising Sentences

● **Rewrite each of the following rambling or run-on sentences as two or more separate sentences. Take out any unnecessary words.**

1. If you want to learn how to cook, you should begin by buying the proper cookware, including pots, pans, and a grill, as well as utensils like spoons, ladles, and spatulas and also have a pantry full of lots and lots of dried herbs and spices to add fresh, exciting flavors to your foods.

_____

_____

_____

2. Some people prefer grilling outside to cooking indoors, grilling is an entire and complete art of its own that takes much skill and lots of practice.

_____

_____

_____

3. You can attend one of several famous cooking schools that are in existence around the world, many of them specialize in different kinds of foods as well as restaurant management.

_____

_____

_____

4. Vegetarians eat only breads, fruits, vegetables, and also sometimes they eat fish, most people like meat way, way too much to ever give it up for good.

_____

_____

_____

CHAPTER 2

Agreement of Pronouns and Antecedents

● **Rewrite each sentence to correct the pronoun to make it agree with the underlined antecedent.**

1. <u>Devon and Jared</u> were late to class, but he will make up the time at break.

   _____

2. <u>Alicia's friend Sue</u> is back from Italy, and they have many interesting stories to tell.

   _____

3. <u>Troy</u> is the best athlete I know, but it doesn't want to try out for any teams.

   _____

4. I don't know why those <u>stories</u> were deleted, because I think it was good.

   _____

5. <u>Rachel and Stella</u> gave a great presentation, but, unfortunately, we forgot the slides.

   _____

6. Our prize <u>poodle</u> won Most Talented, but they failed to win first prize.

   _____

7. We wanted to invite <u>Ms. Washington</u>, but we didn't know how to contact them.

   _____

8. The <u>mailbox</u> is next to the driveway; don't forget to check her every night.

   _____

● **Use each pronoun in a compound sentence. Be sure each pronoun has an antecedent with which it agrees.**

9. he _____

   _____

10. she _____

   _____

11. it _____

   _____

   _____

CHAPTER 2 Interrogative Pronouns and Demonstrative Pronouns

● **Write the correct interrogative or demonstrative pronoun to complete each grammar rule.**

what	whom	whose	this	who
these	those	that	which	

This interrogative pronoun . . .

1. refers to persons. It is often the subject in a question. _____

2. refers to persons. It is the object of a verb. _____

3. is used when asking about possession. _____

4. is used when asking about a group or class. _____

5. refers to persons. It is the object of a preposition. _____

6. is used for asking about things. _____

7. is used for seeking information. _____

This demonstrative pronoun . . .

8. points out something singular that is near. _____

9. points out something plural that is near. _____

10. points out something singular that is distant. _____

11. points out something plural that is distant. _____

CHAPTER 2 Roots

● **Study the roots in the box below. Then complete each sentence with a word based on your knowledge of these roots. (Hint: You will not use all the roots.)**

vac = empty	phys = body	bio = life	terra = earth
chrono = time	tox = poison	civ = citizen	vis = see
arch = old	hydro = water	grat = pleasing	meter = measure
script = write	neg = no	brev = short	tempo = time

1. _____ is the study of ancient ruins and fossils.

2. A _____ studies living things.

3. Any poisonous substance is said to be _____.

4. Any person who sees well has good _____.

5. We use a _____ to measure temperature.

6. An unoccupied apartment is _____.

7. A book is a written _____ before it is published.

8. Instead of saying "no," a robot might say, "_____."

9. To thank someone for a kind act is to show _____.

10. An _____ is a shortened form of a word.

CHAPTER
2

Relative Pronouns

● **Underline the relative pronoun in each sentence. List each antecedent in the column at the right.**

Antecedent

1. The yams that we ate with dinner gave me a stomachache. _____

2. The electric oven, which was bought last week, is broken. _____

3. *Ulysses*, which is a well-known book, can be challenging to read. _____

4. Ryan, who works at the animal shelter, is planning to be a veterinarian. _____

5. The lifelong friends whose craft store this is made this quilt. _____

6. Megan asked Olivia, whom she greatly admired, to be a mentor. _____

7. The oranges that we picked made a jug of delicious orange juice. _____

8. Tia and Sara, who were prima ballerinas, own a dance studio. _____

9. The snow, which came down all night, covered our cars. _____

10. Trains that pass by our house have very loud whistles. _____

11. Is this the elephant that can do all the funny tricks? _____

12. The people who were cast in *Our Town* know a lot about Thornton Wilder. _____

13. The sonnet that was read aloud reflected Shakespeare's style. _____

● **Now enter the first letter of each antecedent on the corresponding line below. If your answers are correct, you will reveal the answer to this riddle.**

The more of them you take, the more you leave behind. What are they?

Answer: __ __ __ __   __ __ __ __ __ __ __ __ __
         1   2   3   4   5   6   7   8   9 10 11 12 13

CHAPTER
2 Indefinite Pronouns

● **Circle the indefinite pronoun in each sentence.**

1. Much of what we know about our universe comes from the telescope.

2. Long ago nobody believed that Earth revolved around the sun.

3. Someone had to invent an instrument that allowed people to see the planets up close.

4. The planets revolve around the sun, each at its own speed.

5. Everything in the heavens looks closer than it actually is.

6. When a star dies, another will likely take its place.

7. There is something exciting and mysterious about space.

8. Thanks to Galileo, everybody knows that the sun is the center of our universe.

9. Is there anyone in the world who is not fascinated by stargazing?

10. To me, nothing sounds more exciting than riding in a spaceship.

11. Among my friends, few think humans will eventually live on the moon.

12. Some in the scientific community believe that there was once life on Mars.

CHAPTER 2 Dictionary

● **Find each word in a dictionary. Write the part of each word's entry that is written on the chart. The first one is done for you.**

Word	Entry Part
1. shower	1. Sample Usage _He took a shower after the game._

Word	Entry Part
2. nettle	2. Etymology

Word	Entry Part
3. surf casting	3. Word Definition

Word	Entry Part
4. martensite	4. Part of Speech

Word	Entry Part
5. dominate	5. Pronunciation

Name of Dictionary: _____

Agreement with Indefinite Pronouns

CHAPTER 2

● **Underline the indefinite pronoun and circle the verb in each sentence. If the verb is correct, write *correct* on the line. If the verb is incorrect, write the correct verb on the line.**

1. Some offers educational programs on whales. _____

2. Nobody from the three groups want to miss this field trip. _____

3. Several is interested in reptiles. _____

4. Everyone hopes the team will arrive soon. _____

5. Much is out of our reach. _____

6. All is waiting to see the school play. _____

7. Few works as lifeguards this year. _____

8. Others walks in the gardens. _____

9. Everybody receives extra credit. _____

10. Many are writing reports about their summer vacations. _____

11. Either of the posters are acceptable. _____

12. Nothing about these suggestions excite the students more than planning a field trip! _____

Self-Assessment

● Check *Always, Sometimes,* or *Never* to respond to each statement.

Writing	Always	Sometimes	Never
I can identify a how-to article and its features.			
I can write clear, concise steps in logical order, provide appropriate details, and omit unnecessary information.			
I can trim rambling or run-on sentences, making every word count.			
I can identify roots and use them to understand the meaning of words.			
I can identify and use all the parts of a dictionary entry.			
I can include all the key features when I write a how-to article.			

Grammar	Always	Sometimes	Never
I can identify and use the correct pronoun to show person, number, and gender.			
I can identify and use subject pronouns.			
I can identify and use object pronouns.			
I can choose the correct pronoun to use after *than* and *as*.			
I can identify and use possessive pronouns.			
I can identify and use intensive and reflexive pronouns.			
I can show agreement between pronouns and their antecedents.			
I can identify and use interrogative and demonstrative pronouns.			
I can identify and use relative pronouns.			
I can identify and use indefinite pronouns.			
I can show agreement between indefinite pronouns and verbs.			

● Write the most useful thing you learned in this chapter.

_____

_____

CHAPTER

3

Principal Parts of Verbs

● Write *past, past participle,* or *present participle* to identify each
   italicized verb. Then underline the auxiliary verbs in five sentences.
   The first one is done for you.

1. The storm <u>had</u> *flown* in more quickly than we expected.   _past participle_

2. Rashad and I *ran* home from school to take shelter.   _____

3. We saw that the storm had *blown* down a tree in front
   of our house.   _____

4. Luckily, the tree *missed* our neighbor's car.   _____

5. Rashad was *telling* me to make certain that all the
   windows were closed.   _____

6. Together we secured the house before the storm
   grew worse.   _____

7. That morning we had *seen* on the TV news that there
   might be a tornado warning.   _____

8. Neither Rashad nor I *knew* what a tornado was really like.   _____

9. We *decided* that the safest place in the house was
   the basement.   _____

10. The storm was *raging* for hours, but we never saw
    a tornado.   _____

● **Now write a few sentences about an amusing or an unusual experience**
   you've had related to weather. Use at least two verbs in the present
   participle form and circle them.

_____

_____

_____

_____

CHAPTER 3
Transitive and Intransitive Verbs

- **Identify the underlined verb in each sentence by writing *transitive* or *intransitive* on the line.**

  1. In the fall millions of monarchs <u>fly</u> south.   _____

  2. A female monarch <u>lays</u> about 400 eggs at one time.   _____

  3. A newborn monarch caterpillar can <u>eat</u> its own weight
     in food.   _____

  4. Ladybugs <u>use</u> their feet to smell.   _____

  5. They <u>chew</u> from side to side, not up and down.   _____

  6. Ladybugs <u>nibble</u> aphids off rosebushes.   _____

  7. To chirp, male crickets <u>rub</u> their wings together.   _____

  8. Female crickets cannot <u>chirp</u> at all.   _____

  9. Many animals <u>eat</u> crickets, including spiders, frogs,
     and birds.   _____

  10. Some spiders <u>spin</u> webs that are stronger than steel!   _____

  11. Many spiders <u>live</u> in dark spaces.   _____

  12. Most spiders' poisons will not <u>harm</u> people.   _____

- **Now go back and read each sentence again. Circle the doer and underline the receiver (if there is one).**

What Makes a Good Business Letter?

● **The following business letter includes several errors. Use proofreading marks to revise it. You should find three errors in capitalization, three errors in punctuation, and one error in spelling. There are also two examples of informal or incorrect usage. Replace these words with more appropriate language.**

Jackson Junior High
33445 oak Drive
Chicago, IL 12345
(123) 555-0099

Mr James Ruff
Wagging Tails Pet Sitting
dogtown IL 12344
(123) 555-8833

Dear Mr. Ruff;

We would like to thank you for visiting our class last week to talk about your experiences in the pet-sitting business. We enjoyed hearing about your adventures in dealing with all kinds of owners and their animals, especially the potbellied pig! In fact, we would like to include a monthly column about pets in our school newspaper.

If it ain't too much trouble, each month we would like to send a student to interview you. The columns could include tips for pet care, special animal stories, or information about animal health and training. In exchange for your generosity, we would be happy to help your business by placing an ad in our newspaper.

Please contact us at the phone number above if you would be interested in becoming part of our school newspaper. Thanks again for taking the time to share your knowledge and great pet stories. We look forward to hearing from ya.

Sincerly,

Ms. Garcia

Ms. garcia and the Students of Room 12
8th Grade Class
Jackson Junior High

CHAPTER 3 Troublesome Verbs

● **Circle the verb that correctly completes each sentence.**

1. I will (**si**t   se**t**) the box in this corner.

2. Ahmed will (lea**r**n   tea**c**h) me how to use the new computer.

3. The campers have (risen   raised) early to start their long hike.

4. I have (**l**aid   l**ai**n) clean towels on the counter for you.

5. (**B**ring   Tak**e**) your report card home for your parents to sign.

6. He accidentally (let   left) his coat at the restaurant.

7. Brett (**b**orrowed   lent) me his tools so I could fix my car.

8. Krista (learned   taught) about the Civil War in Mr. Smith's class.

9. Please (**r**ise   **r**aise) the flag first every morning.

10. You may (set   sit) in the chair by the window.

● **Go back and find the letter in bold type in each word you circled. Write these letters on the lines below. If your answers are correct, you will find the answer to this riddle.**

I am the beginning of sorrow and the end of sickness.
You cannot express happiness without me. I am always
in risk, yet never in danger.

Answer: ___ ___ ___   ___ ___ ___ ___ ___ ___   ___
           1   2   3   4   5   6   7   8   9   10

CHAPTER 3

Linking Verbs

● **Circle eight linking verbs in the following paragraph. Then underline ten subject complements. (Hint: Subject complements are nouns, pronouns, or adjectives; they can be one word or a group of words.)**

    This morning the sky appeared clear, blue, and sunny. I imagine that the sun on my back and the wind in my hair feel wonderful! Today seems perfect for a trip to the beach. Today, however, I am in school. As I sit here daydreaming about the beach, the air smells fresh and the water tastes salty. The waves even sound thunderous in my ears. I could stay in this daydream forever, until I realize that the whole class is staring at me. My face grows hot. I guess I was asleep!

● **What subject complements did you identify above? Find and circle these words in the word search below. Words can go across, down, or diagonally.**

```
O  R  T  A  W  C  X  L  B  S  I  E
S  F  R  E  S  H  R  A  U  P  E  C
A  T  H  U  D  J  H  O  T  D  R  M
L  S  C  L  E  A  R  A  L  O  P  K
T  Q  U  Y  G  E  B  N  N  P  E  R
Y  C  A  L  D  I  E  L  S  P  R  W
S  W  O  N  D  E  R  F  U  L  F  D
H  T  U  S  E  U  A  H  N  E  E  G
M  H  I  O  A  S  N  E  N  R  C  H
T  X  A  S  L  E  E  P  Y  I  T  Y
```

CHAPTER 3

Purpose and Tone

- **Read the body paragraph from a business letter. Then write details that support the writer's purpose in the Cause-and-Effect graphic organizer. For an example of a completed Cause-and-Effect chart, see page 140.**

Big Sky Airlines is the most horrible airline I have ever flown. I would like to get a refund of my ticket. I was disgusted that I had to ask three times before the flight attendant finally brought me something to drink. I was appalled at how rude he was to me. And then, no one seemed to have accurate information about gates and times for our arrival. We left two hours late. As I said, I would like a refund of my ticket because the entire experience was disastrous.

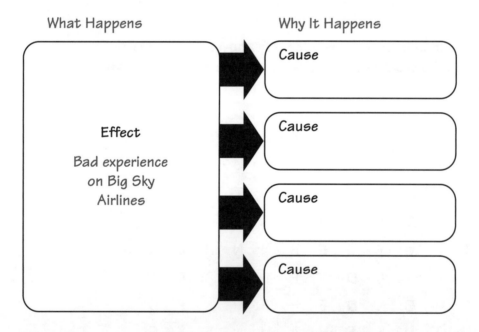

What Happens

Effect

Bad experience
on Big Sky
Airlines

Why It Happens

Cause

Cause

Cause

Cause

- **Now go back to the paragraph and circle four words that might seem too harsh for a respectful, professional business letter. On another sheet of paper, rewrite the paragraph, using your graphic organizer as a guide. Remember to use appropriate words and a courteous tone.**

© Loyola Press

Active and Passive Voices

● **If the sentence is in the active voice, rewrite it in the passive voice. If the sentence is in the passive voice, rewrite it in the active voice.**

1. Leonardo da Vinci, a man of many talents, painted the *Mona Lisa*.

   _____

2. The famous *Last Supper* was also painted by Leonardo da Vinci.

   _____

3. The Louvre museum in Paris, France, displays the *Mona Lisa*.

   _____

4. Da Vinci's notes for inventions and other ideas were written backward.

   _____

5. The Renaissance ushered in a period of rebirth in art and learning.

   _____

6. The moons of Jupiter were discovered by the Renaissance
   astronomer Galileo.

   _____

7. The telescope was improved by Galileo.

   _____

8. Galileo believed that the sun was the center of the universe.

   _____

9. During this time it was accepted by most people that the sun
   revolved around the earth.

   _____

10. Galileo discovered four of Jupiter's moons.

   _____

CHAPTER
3

Simple, Progressive, and Perfect Tenses

● **Underline the verb or verb phrase in each sentence. Write the letter that identifies the tense of the verb or verb phrase. Write *present, past,* or *future* to identify the action each one expresses. The first one is done for you.**

a. Simple tense   b. Progressive tense   c. Perfect tense

1. My brother <u>studies</u> every night for two hours.   _a_   _present_

2. The store will be closing at nine o'clock.   _____   _____

3. We are preparing for next week's competition.   _____   _____

4. The candidates have posted the signs for the election.   _____   _____

5. Our class will visit the museum at the end of the month.   _____   _____

6. John has purchased a new tire for his bicycle.   _____   _____

7. The chores will have been finished by the time I get home.   _____   _____

8. Amy will have read five books by the end of summer.   _____   _____

9. The researchers presented their findings at a public hearing.   _____   _____

10. We will be working together on the science project.   _____   _____

11. I was selling tickets for the student talent show.   _____   _____

12. The issue has been discussed at several meetings recently.   _____   _____

● **Now go back and place a check next to each sentence that includes a verb in the passive voice.**

Adjective and Adverb Clauses

CHAPTER 3

● **Rewrite each sentence by adding an adjective clause to modify the italicized nouns. Remember that an adjective clause usually begins with a relative pronoun such as *who, whom, whose, which,* or *that.* Circle the relative pronouns in your new sentences.**

1. The *product* was less effective than advertised.

_____

2. Your *staff* provided every luxury we desired.

_____

3. The *hotel* was more beautiful than we ever imagined.

_____

4. I am available to speak with you at any *time*.

_____

● **Rewrite each sentence by adding an adverb clause to modify the italicized verbs. Remember that an adverb clause usually begins with a subordinate conjunction such as *than, until, because, after, before, although, as, as if,* or *unless.* Circle the subordinate conjunctions in your new sentences.**

5. Before the trip started, the tour guide *spoke*.

_____

6. We weren't hungry, but we *ate*.

_____

7. The product *should be replaced*.

_____

8. You *can watch* the game.

_____

CHAPTER 3

Indicative and Imperative Moods

● Underline the verb or verb phrase in each sentence. Circle *indicative* or *imperative* to identify the mood each verb or verb phrase expresses. Then, if the sentence is indicative, rewrite it as imperative. If the sentence is imperative, rewrite it as indicative. Your new sentences can vary in meaning from the original sentences.

1. Join us for the picnic on Sunday.   indicative   imperative

   _____

2. We are planning a trip to Chile this summer.   indicative   imperative

   _____

3. Has Wags eaten all the food in his bowl?   indicative   imperative

   _____

4. Please bring the necessary supplies to class.   indicative   imperative

   _____

5. Place the birthday gifts on this table.   indicative   imperative

   _____

6. Jana is playing varsity tennis this year.   indicative   imperative

   _____

● In the space below, sketch two people talking. Use speech bubbles, as in a comic book. Show one person asking a question in the indicative mood and the other answering in the imperative mood.

© Loyola Press

CHAPTER 3

Subjunctive Mood

● **Circle the correct word choice in each sentence. Not all sentences have verbs in the subjunctive mood.**

1. The director said it is necessary that the cast (show   shows) up on time.

2. I wish I (was   were) on the stage crew instead of in the chorus line.

3. The stage manager doesn't require that the crew (be   are) on hand all the time.

4. I know that the stage manager wouldn't be angry if I (was   were) late once in a while.

5. I am going to request that I (be   am) given time off work at the pet shelter when I'm desperately needed there.

6. My mother says that a good deed (count   counts) toward character building.

● **For each picture write a sentence that includes a verb in the subjunctive mood. Remember that the subjunctive mood refers to what is hoped or wished rather than what actually is.**

7. _____
_____
_____

8. _____
_____
_____

9. _____
_____
_____

10. _____
_____
_____

11. _____
_____
_____

12. _____
_____
_____

CHAPTER 3

Compound Words and Clipped Words

● **Write the clipped form of each word below.**

1. influenza _____

2. automobile _____

3. rhinoceros _____

4. laboratory _____

5. combination _____

6. necktie _____

7. refrigerator _____

8. mathematics _____

9. statistics _____

10. draperies _____

11. dormitory _____

12. preparatory _____

13. graduate _____

14. doctor _____

15. delicatessen _____

● **Circle the correct form of the compound word to complete each sentence. Consult a dictionary as needed.**

16. Jessica is my (five year old   five-year-old) little sister.

17. My uncle taught me how to play (football   foot-ball) last summer.

18. How many (brother in laws   brothers-in-law) do you have?

19. That documentary was a real (eye opener   eye-opener).

20. This (snowstorm   snow storm) is the worst I've ever experienced.

21. Did Grandma lend you her favorite (cook book   cookbook)?

22. We cheered as the (fourth quarter   fourth-quarter) score flashed on the board.

23. Well, that's not something you see (every day   everyday)!

24. We will plant a row of (forget me nots   forget-me-nots) along the wall.

● **Draw a Compare and Contrast chart like the one on page 138 to compare the words *influenza* and *flu* on a separate sheet of paper.**

3 Modal Auxiliaries

● **Use the modal auxiliaries in the box to write sentences on the given topics. Write the sentences as indicated in parentheses, using the underlined verbs. The first one is done for you.**

may	might	can	could
must	should	will	would

1. Topic: <u>Study</u>ing for a midterm (necessity, present tense)

   I must study for my midterm this weekend. _____

2. Topic: <u>Clean</u>ing your room (obligation, past tense)

   _____

3. Topic: <u>Watch</u>ing a movie (possibility, past tense)

   _____

4. Topic: <u>Play</u>ing a soccer game (ability, present tense)

   _____

5. Topic: <u>Borrow</u>ing a sweater (permission, present tense)

   _____

6. Topic: <u>Shop</u>ping for a gift (intention, future tense)

   _____

7. Topic: <u>Finish</u>ing a task (possibility, past tense)

   _____

8. Topic: <u>Follow</u>ing directions (necessity, present tense)

   _____

9. Topic: <u>Cook</u>ing a meal (possibility, present tense)

   _____

10. Topic: <u>Finish</u>ing your homework (necessity, present tense)

   _____

CHAPTER 3

Agreement of Subject and Verb—Part I

- **Correct the subject-verb agreement problems in the sentences below by writing the correct form of the italicized verb on the line. If the sentence is correct as is, write *correct*.**

1. *Was* you living here during the Northridge earthquake? _____

2. Most people *doesn't* know what to do during an earthquake. _____

3. *There are* several wildfires raging in those dry hills. _____

4. A good place to hide during a tornado *are* the basement. _____

5. Hurricanes, as well as thunderstorms, *is* common in Florida. _____

6. *There's been* many hurricanes in Louisiana as well. _____

7. Overflowing of rivers *creates* flooding in some areas. _____

8. *Are* you aware that a tsunami can follow an earthquake? _____

9. Oklahoma, a Midwestern state, *experience* many tornadoes. _____

10. I *doesn't* know which state gets the most snowfall each year. _____

11. *Were* you able to obtain an earthquake safety manual? _____

12. *There is* several commonsense rules one should know. _____

13. One state with historic snowfalls *are* South Dakota. _____

14. Alaska *don't* get sunshine during certain times of the year. _____

15. Lightning may often *strikes* without warning. _____

- **Now go back and underline the subject of each italicized verb.**

CHAPTER 3

Completing Forms and Writing Checks

● **Fill out the check as directed.**

On July 10, 2005, Lauren Simms bought a pair of in-line skates for $65.99. She bought them at a store called Wild Wheels. She paid with a personal check.

Lauren Simms	808
404 Shady Tree Lane	
Hidden Oaks, TN 12233	_____20_____ 4-8/310

PAY TO THE
ORDER OF _____ $ _____

_____ Dollars

UNIVERSAL BANK
Hidden Oaks, TN 12234

For _____   _____

000   1111   22   333   444   5   678

● **Complete this store return form for two CDs. You ordered the CDs on October 5, 2005. CD #1 was damaged in shipment. CD #2 was not the CD you ordered. You would like to receive store credit for both CDs.**

STORE RETURN FORM

MOSTLY MUSIC, Ashland, OR
Merchandise Return Form   Date: _____

Billing Address: **Shipping Address (if different from billing):**

Full Name: _____   Full Name: _____

Street Address: _____   Street Address: _____

City/State/ZIP: _____   City/State/ZIP: _____

Date Merchandise Purchased: _____

Title of Product #1: _____   Qty: _____   Price Each: _____

Title of Product #2: _____   Qty: _____   Price Each: _____

                                                        Total Price: _____

Why are you returning the merchandise?

Product #1: _____

Product #2: _____

Would you like a refund, store credit, or replacement product(s)?

(circle one)   REFUND   CREDIT   REPLACEMENT

Signed: _____

Agreement of Subject and Verb—Part II

CHAPTER 3

● **Circle the verb in parentheses that correctly completes each sentence.**

1. My mom and dad (is   are) taking us on a trip to Europe.

2. Each of us (seems   seem) interested in visiting a different country.

3. My family (travels   travel) somewhere new each summer.

4. Another place we'd really like to visit (is   are) China.

5. One of the museums we may (visits   visit) is the Louvre in Paris.

6. My family and I (leave   leaves) the first week of July.

7. Neither my brother nor I (have   has) been out of the United States.

8. Everyone (experience   experiences) many new and exciting adventures.

9. Germany and Spain (are   is) the countries of our ancestry.

10. Each of us (need   needs) to get new clothes for the trip.

11. Spanish language and culture (was   were) my mom's major in college.

12. Our tour group (chooses   choose) which cities to explore.

13. Two things my dad wants to see (is   are) the Eiffel Tower and Big Ben.

14. Many of us (enjoy   enjoys) trying different ethnic foods.

● **Now go back to the even-numbered items. Underline the first letter of each word you circled and write the letters below to answer this riddle:**

What will you break every time you name it?

Answer: ___ ___ ___ ___ ___ ___ ___
         2   4   6   8   10   12   14

Name_____ Date_____

Self-Assessment

● Check *Always*, *Sometimes*, or *Never* to respond to each statement.

Writing	Always	Sometimes	Never
I can identify a business letter and its features.			
I can identify and write all the parts of a business letter, including the date, addresses, salutation, body, closing, signature, and references.			
I can identify adjective and adverb clauses and use them to enhance my writing.			
I can identify compound words and clipped words and spell them correctly.			
I can correctly fill out checks and business forms.			
I can use the appropriate tone for a business letter, making sure to be courteous, detailed, and persuasive.			

Grammar	Always	Sometimes	Never
I can identify the principal parts of verbs.			
I can identify and use transitive and intransitive verbs.			
I can identify troublesome verbs and use them correctly.			
I can identify and use linking verbs.			
I can identify and use verbs in the active and passive voices.			
I can identify and use verbs in the simple, progressive, and perfect tenses.			
I can identify and use verbs in the indicative, imperative, and subjunctive moods.			
I can identify and use modal auxiliaries.			
I can identify and use correct subject and verb agreement.			

● **What was the most helpful thing you learned in this chapter?**

_____

_____

CHAPTER 4

Participles

- **Underline the participial phrase in each sentence. Then write *present,* *past,* or *perfect* on the line to identify the tense.**

1. Galloping over the hill, the chestnut stallion looks magnificent. _____

2. The girl waiting by the door is my sister. _____

3. Having been given a second chance, I read the speech perfectly. _____

4. Hiding under the chair, the fuzzy kitten took a long nap. _____

5. Hit with a baseball, the window shattered into hundreds of pieces. _____

6. Kibble, having eaten the carrot, retired to the back of his cage. _____

7. Having lost the game, we realized that the team needed more practice. _____

8. Fiona gazed at the sun setting over the mountaintops. _____

9. Cheering loudly, Keisha saw the team score another touchdown. _____

10. The river flowing through the town was dangerously high. _____

11. Loved by its new family, the stray dog had finally found a home. _____

12. The parrot, having been taught to speak, mimicked everyone. _____

- **Now go back and circle the noun or pronoun each participial phrase describes.**

CHAPTER 4 Placement of Participles

- **Identify the participle in each sentence and write it on the line. Then circle the letter in your answer that corresponds with the number. The first one is done for you.**

1. One-third of the world's required oxygen supply is provided by rain forests.   _required_ 8

2. Little light filters through the swaying trees of the canopy.   _____ 5

3. Chirping squirrel monkeys swing from branches overhead.   _____ 1

4. Slithering snakes hunt for food.   _____ 4

5. Many surviving species receive the protection of local laws.   _____ 5

6. A rain forest's covered environment is warm and moist.   _____ 2

7. Big cats, like the jaguar, prefer to rest in hidden places during the day.   _____ 6

8. Most laws of protection have brought about the results wanted.   _____ 2

9. The endangered mandrill is almost extinct in central Africa.   _____ 8

10. High in the trees, a yelping toucan communicates with other birds.   _____ 1

- **Write the letters you circled, in order, on the lines below. If your answers are correct, you will reveal the answer to the riddle.**

In what place does yesterday always follow today?

Answer: ___ ___ ___ ___ ___ ___ ___ ___ ___ ___

- **Rewrite each sentence to correct the dangling or misplaced participle.**

11. Wet from the storm, I allowed our dog to come into the house.

_____

12. Hurrying to get to class on time, the door was already closed.

_____

CHAPTER 4

What Makes a Good Description?

● **Read the descriptive paragraph. Then answer the questions.**

The kitchen was the heart and soul of Ana's home. It was the gathering place. This was where Ana's mama prepared love for all to share. Ana sat quietly on her stool by the counter and watched Mama move about the kitchen. Mama's slender fingers were a blur as she chopped, grated, and sliced. In her skilled, caring hands, food wasn't cooked; it was created. She didn't prepare dishes; she created masterpieces. Mama moved gracefully around the kitchen like a dancer, her long skirt swishing softly around her legs with each step. Ana watched as Mama grated fresh nutmeg into a bowl of creamy sauce. The warm air almost burst with the sweet fragrances of fresh herbs and hot spices. Boiling sauces popped softly on the stove, while onions, garlic, and peppers sizzled in a pan. Ana's mama looked up at her and smiled a knowing smile. Ana knew that one day she would dance in the kitchen, just like her mama.

1. What is the mood of this passage? Why do you think so?

   _____

   _____

2. How does the writer help you see, smell, and hear what is happening in Mama's kitchen? Write precise words that create these images.

   I see _____

   _____ .

   I smell _____ .

   I hear _____ .

3. How did this passage make you feel?

   _____

4. Name one comparison the writer uses to create a vivid image. Do you feel it was an effective comparison?

   _____

   _____

CHAPTER 4

Gerunds as Subjects and Complements

● **Look at each picture. Then use a gerund or a gerund phrase to complete each sentence and describe the picture.**

1. Dexter's favorite game is _____.

2. _____ is one sport Lena loves.

3. _____ is a wonderful experience.

4. _____ is Lauren's greatest talent.

5. _____ is the path to good grades.

6. Dustin's dream is _____.

● **Now go back and read your sentences. Write *S* or *SC* on the line to identify your gerund or gerund phrase as a subject or a subject complement.**

CHAPTER 4

Gerunds as Objects and Appositives

● Underline the gerund phrase in each sentence. Then circle the gerund.
Identify how the gerund is used by writing *DO* (direct object), *OP*
(object of a preposition), or *A* (appositive) on the line.

1. Many people do not like giving speeches in front of large groups. _____

2. Tanya exercises by swimming 30 laps every morning. _____

3. Jared enjoys watching football on Sunday afternoons. _____

4. Aerobics, exercising to music, is a popular workout at most gyms. _____

5. Amanda loves throwing parties on the weekends. _____

6. Trey's talent, acting in the community theater, will take him far someday. _____

7. Are you the one who started using that nickname for me? _____

8. I didn't know math skills could lead to getting so many interesting jobs. _____

9. Jeremy began his research by reading books about motorcycles. _____

10. Min tried drawing portraits of people rather than animals. _____

● Find and circle the gerunds you identified above in the word search
below. They can go across, down, or diagonally.

```
E  U  T  H  R  O  W  I  N  G  A  T
X  A  S  O  G  E  T  T  I  N  G  W
E  X  U  I  I  X  A  A  B  O  G  A
R  I  N  O  N  E  C  D  G  N  E  T
C  G  H  S  N  G  T  N  I  D  G  C
I  S  W  I  M  M  I  N  G  N  F  H
S  C  E  X  T  W  N  E  I  X  G  I
I  B  R  M  A  I  G  V  N  J  A  N
N  E  O  R  U  C  I  W  T  I  N  G
G  X  D  S  A  G  P  I  N  G  R  E
```

CHAPTER 4

Organization

● **Read each description. Write *chronological, spatial, order of importance*, or *comparison and contrast* to tell how each description is organized. Then explain your answer.**

1. I could feel the excitement building as the game progressed. My heart was pounding so loud in my ears, I thought I would explode from the adrenaline. As I stood out in center field, I raised my face to gaze up at the clear, blue, cloudless sky. I wanted to laugh and cry at the same time. After 25 long years, our school was going to win the playoffs. I watched, spellbound, as the last pitch was thrown—strike three! The crowd exploded like a box of Fourth of July fireworks. We did it!

   Type of Organization: _____

   How do you know? _____

2. Maui and her twin sister, Leah, are quite different. Because they are twins you would think they would be similar. Not true! Maui is a natural artist; she loves to create with her hands through painting and sketching. Leah is a natural athlete. She'd rather swing a tennis racquet or spike a volleyball than sit in front of a sketch pad. Both girls, however, enjoy reading mysteries, riding horses, and going to the beach.

   Type of Organization: _____

   How do you know? _____

● **Write the two types of organization that are not shown in the descriptions above.**

   3. _____   4. _____

● **On a separate sheet of paper, write two descriptive paragraphs, one using each type of organization that you named on the lines above. Choose from these topics: your best friend's face, an exciting sporting event, a great party, the outside of the school.**

CHAPTER 4

Possessives with Gerunds, Using *-ing* Verb Forms

● **Circle the word that correctly completes each sentence.**

1. (Amy Amy's) taking an earlier flight gave her more time for sightseeing.

2. (Your You) lending me this book will save me a trip to the library.

3. (Us Our) visiting Alaska was the whole family's decision.

4. I thought (John John's) helping to create the Web site showed his commitment to the project.

5. I hope that (my me) studying hard for this exam will result in a good grade.

● **Write four different sentences using the word *winning*. Use the word as a gerund (G), a participle in a participial phrase (PP), a simple participial adjective (PA), and a progressive tense verb (PV). For example, using the word *calling*:**

Gerund: *Calling my family* is what makes me feel good when I'm down.
Participle in a participial phrase: The person *calling from downstairs* was my father.
Participial adjective: Many people use *calling cards* to make long-distance phone calls.
Progressive tense verb (past): I *was calling* my dog to come inside the house.

Winning	How is the word used?
_____	_____
_____	
_____	_____
_____	
_____	_____
_____	
_____	_____
_____	

CHAPTER 4

Infinitives as Subjects and Complements

- **In each sentence underline the infinitive phrase. Circle the infinitive in each phrase. Then write *S* (subject) or *SC* (subject complement) to identify how the infinitive phrase is used.**

1. An incredible act of kindness is to adopt a stray animal. _____

2. Our dream is to explore all the countries of Africa. _____

3. To have a working knowledge of computers is essential. _____

4. For instance, to type on a typewriter is basically obsolete. _____

5. To go to college is a must in my family. _____

6. My plan is to attend one of the Ivy League universities. _____

7. To learn a new language is challenging but rewarding. _____

8. My idea was to offer more tutoring programs after school. _____

9. Mina's greatest achievement was to complete her Ph.D. _____

10. To cook all kinds of ethnic foods is my favorite hobby. _____

- **Complete each sentence with an infinitive.**

11. Something I would like to achieve is

_____.

12. _____

is one of my family's traditions.

© Loyola Press

CHAPTER
4

Graphic Organizers

● Use the Venn diagram to compare and contrast elementary school
and junior high school. Write ideas that apply only to elementary
school in the larger section of the left circle. Write ideas that apply
only to junior high in the larger section of the right circle. Write the
ways both schools are the same in the overlapping middle section.

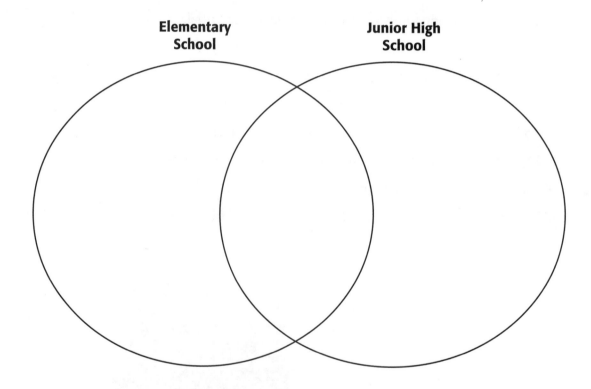

**Elementary
School**

**Junior High
School**

● On a separate sheet of paper, write a paragraph comparing
elementary school to junior high. Use the ideas from your
Venn diagram.

CHAPTER 4

Infinitives as Objects

● **Underline the infinitive in each sentence. Then circle the verb of which it is the direct object.**

1. Mr. Hale encouraged us to brainstorm ideas for the club's fundraiser.

2. Shyla's horse started to gallop at full speed over the rocky pathway.

3. Our kittens decided to escape the rain by hiding under the house.

4. We mean to find old letters and journals in my grandparents' attic.

5. Tom expects to be the first runner across the finish line.

6. Mia wanted to alleviate the sick child's discomfort.

7. How did you manage to finish all that paperwork?

8. My sister needed me to help her with a special birthday dinner.

9. After practice, he likes to exercise for several hours in the gym.

● **Write each infinitive below in a complete sentence. Use each infinitive as a direct object.**

10. to climb _____

_____

11. to sing _____

_____

12. to be _____

_____

© Loyola Press

Infinitives as Appositives

CHAPTER 4

- **From the list below, choose the appositive that best completes each sentence. Then circle the noun it explains.**

Infinitive Choices

R. to become a professional ice skater

E. to win the district championship

I. to procrastinate constantly

D. to interview our grandparents

N. to make balloon animals

H. to sell everything at 50 percent off

A. to give an oral report

C. to construct a new hospital

G. to take roll at the beginning of class

1. It was her ultimate dream ———.

2. Our team's hope, _____, was finally achieved.

3. The builders' plan, _____, was stopped by local landowners.

4. Mr. Greer's assignment, _____, helped us learn about history.

5. My tendency _____ means that I must rush to meet deadlines.

6. Our carnival booth's activity, _____, delighted all the children.

7. It is Daniel's turn _____.

8. Our final reduction, _____, helped to empty the store.

9. Her biggest fear, _____, was overcome by taking a speech class.

- **Now write the letters on the lines below. If your answers are correct, you will reveal the answer to the riddle.**

What do you have when 20 rabbits step backward?

Answer: A ___ ___ ___ E ___ ___ ___ ___ ___ ___ R E L I N E!
        1 2 3   4 5 6 7   8 9

CHAPTER

4 Thesaurus

● **Use a thesaurus to find a more precise or vivid word to replace each underlined word.**

Did you know that animals traveled into space before people did? It's true! Animals led the way in space exploration. Scientists wanted to make certain that animals could (1) <u>live</u> in space before humans attempted the trip. The first animals to survive a (2) <u>trip</u> into space were a monkey and eleven mice. They rode in a rocket straight up into space and down again. The mission was a success. The most (3) <u>well-known</u> animal of all, however, is Ham the chimpanzee. He actually (4) <u>worked</u> for his mission by learning how to pull certain levers during the space flight. Each time he correctly pulled a lever, he would (5) <u>get</u> a banana pellet!

1. _____

2. _____

3. _____

4. _____

5. _____

● **Circle the word in parentheses that best replaces the underlined word in each sentence. Look up any words you don't understand in a dictionary to make sure you choose the most accurate word.**

6. Tera felt <u>weak</u> after not eating all day. (fragile   frail   soft)

7. Jamal <u>gave</u> many hours to volunteer work. (supplied   granted   contributed)

8. Siena <u>tried</u> to finish the painting before the end of class.
   (struggled   attempted   strained)

9. The <u>crafty</u> fox slid into the henhouse before anyone could see it.
   (cunning   smooth   artful)

10. He awoke, startled and <u>scared</u>, at the sound of the loud crash.
    (intimidated   anxious   frightened)

CHAPTER 4

Infinitives as Adjectives

● **Underline the infinitive phrase used as an adjective in each sentence. Then write the noun or pronoun it describes.**

1. The street to take to the mall goes near our school.   _____

2. She is always the one to bring delicious, homemade desserts.   _____

3. The first reference to consult for maps is an atlas.   _____

4. I bought a ticket to ride the roller coaster at the ticket booth.   _____

5. This health manual outlines a myriad of ways to exercise.   _____

6. The horse to ride in the parade is that beautiful chestnut.   _____

7. The kitten to adopt is the striped one in that big basket.   _____

8. The person to watch in the game is the quarterback.   _____

9. Myra knew she didn't have time to finish the essay.   _____

10. Acceptable guests to invite to the classroom are listed
    on the board.   _____

● **Search a newspaper. Find three infinitive phrases that are used as adjectives. Cut out the articles and underline the phrases. Share them with a partner.**

CHAPTER 4 Infinitives as Adverbs

● **Read the paragraph. Go back and underline six infinitive phrases used as adverbs. Then draw an arrow from each phrase to the verb, adjective, or adverb it describes. Identify the word by writing *V* (verb), *ADJ* (adjective), or *ADV* (adverb) above it.**

Last summer I went to Washington, D.C., to visit our nation's capital. I was thrilled to see many original documents written by presidents of the past. After viewing the Washington monument, I visited the Capitol to learn more about our country's government. It was beautiful! I felt extremely patriotic as I walked the grand hallways. I also visited the White House, and I was excited to see the place where our president and his family live. I listened to the tour guide talk about all the famous people who had stayed there at one time or another. Next, I traveled to the Lincoln Memorial to admire the statue of my favorite president, Abraham Lincoln. I was not in Washington long enough to see everything on my sightseeing list, but I still had a great time!

● **Now write two sentences about one museum, building, monument, or place that you have seen or that you would like to see in Washington, D.C. Include an infinitive used as an adverb in each sentence.**

_____

_____

_____

_____

Figurative Language

CHAPTER 4

- **Write *simile* or *metaphor* to identify the comparison in each sentence. Then underline the two things being compared. The first one is done for you.**

1. My big black <u>cat</u> slithers around my ankles like a <u>snake</u>. _____simile_____

2. She was a graceful swan when she danced. _____

3. The baseball shot out of the park like a rocket. _____

4. Our school was a zoo during graduation ceremonies. _____

5. My skin was as rough as sandpaper after working in the sun. _____

6. My teacher is a hawk circling the classroom during exams. _____

7. Snarling like a lion, the quarterback leapt into the end zone. _____

8. Javier's old dog is still as playful and silly as a young pup. _____

9. Her gentle words were pearls of wisdom to us all. _____

10. Like a bloodhound, he guided us through the thick forest. _____

- **Use hyperbole or personification to write a sentence about each topic.**

11. trees _____

_____

12. baby _____

_____

Voyages in English 8

Hidden and Split Infinitives

CHAPTER 4

● **Find the hidden infinitive in each sentence. Underline the infinitive and circle the word that helped you find it.**

1. Santiago heard the wind whip violently through the treetops.

2. We need not use your truck for our camping trip this weekend.

3. We could see the dancers float about the stage like angels.

4. Can you help me move into my new apartment this weekend?

5. Our dog does not dare enter the house when his paws are muddy.

6. Dad made the neighborhood children clean the yard after their games.

7. Stella does nothing but talk on the phone to her boyfriend.

8. She would prefer to read than participate in sports.

● **Rewrite each sentence to eliminate the split infinitive.**

9. Ms. Cardoza asked me to completely redesign my science project.

_____

10. My brother asked us to not enter his room without knocking.

_____

11. Loc stubbornly decided to not cooperate with the rest of the team.

_____

12. We asked Mom to quickly show us our list of weekend chores.

_____

Name _____ Date _____

Self-Assessment

● Check *Always*, *Sometimes*, or *Never* to respond to each statement.

Writing	Always	Sometimes	Never
I can identify descriptive writing and its features.			
I understand how to effectively organize the details in a descriptive paragraph.			
I can use graphic organizers, such as Venn diagrams and word webs, to organize my ideas.			
I can use a thesaurus to find more vivid and precise words.			
I can identify and use figurative language.			
I include all the key features when I write a description.			

Grammar	Always	Sometimes	Never
I can identify and use participles.			
I can identify and correct dangling and misplaced participles.			
I can identify and use gerunds used as subjects and complements.			
I can identify and use gerunds used as objects and appositives.			
I can identify and use possessives with gerunds.			
I can distinguish gerunds from participles and verbs.			
I can identify and use infinitives as subjects and complements.			
I can identify and use infinitives as objects.			
I can identify and use infinitives as appositives.			
I can identify and use infinitives as adjectives.			
I can identify and use infinitives as adverbs.			
I can identify and use hidden infinitives.			
I can identify and eliminate split infinitives.			

● **Write the most helpful thing you learned in this chapter.**

_____

_____

CHAPTER 5

Types of Adverbs

● **Circle the adverb in each sentence. Then choose its type from the box and write it on the line.**

Types of Adverbs

time	place	manner
degree	affirmation	negation

1. The train moved forward with a screeching jolt. _____

2. We frequently spend time at the beach. _____

3 Cara searched frantically for her lost backpack. _____

4. The spotlight from the helicopter is quite bright. _____

5. The elephants trumpeted loudly as they stampeded. _____

6. Bailey would never catch the football. _____

7. Molly sat there while I practiced my speech. _____

8. The principal's speech was extremely long but entertaining. _____

9. She seldom gets a poor grade on a test. _____

10. I certainly did expect the whole team to attend. _____

11. Handle those valuable ceramics carefully. _____

12. Antonio often gives to charities that help animals. _____

● **Write two sentences about members of your family using adverbs of manner. Circle the adverb in each sentence.**

13. _____

14. _____

CHAPTER 5

Interrogative Adverbs and Adverbial Nouns

● **Underline the adverbial nouns in the sentences.**

1. At the store, we bought eggs and one quart of milk.

2. My teacher allowed 20 minutes to finish the test.

3. We drove more than 1,800 miles across country last summer.

4. We traveled south for the holidays, from Minnesota to Texas.

5. Our plane flew east, carrying us from Oregon to New York.

6. Tyra added two cups of flour to the cookie batter.

7. Our big, fluffy cat weighs 13 pounds.

8. We estimated three feet to each meter.

9. My dad gave us each 75 cents to buy ice cream.

10. The paper clip was so light it didn't even weigh an ounce.

● **Write a conjunction or an interrogative adverb to complete each sentence. Write C for conjunction or I for interrogative on the line.**

11. Tomorrow is the day _____ we hold the annual school Olympics. _____

12. _____ did you place the freshly baked cookies? _____

13. Summer is the time _____ many families take trips. _____

14. This is the building _____ we chose to hold the awards. _____

15. _____ are those students always late to class? _____

CHAPTER 5

What Makes a Good Expository Essay?

- Good expository writing has a main idea clearly stated in a topic sentence. This sentence is then supported by facts, data, statistics, and examples. Read the following paragraph, and then complete the paragraph plan. For an example of a paragraph plan, see page 139.

> The Declaration of Independence, written and signed in 1776, was a revolutionary document for its time. This document declared that the colonies in America were free from British rule. The colonists considered themselves free and independent. The document also stated that the colonists wanted to govern themselves as a new nation. They were declaring their freedom as well as expressing the revolutionary idea that all people have certain rights that cannot be taken away by a government or ruler. The ideas in the Declaration of Independence were seen as so revolutionary that the British claimed the document was treasonous. The Revolutionary War began shortly thereafter.

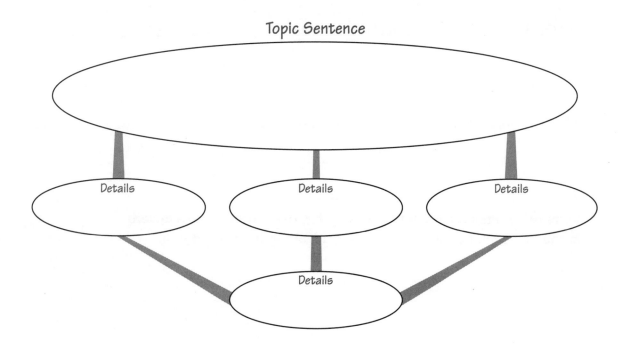

Topic Sentence

Details   Details   Details

Details

© Loyola Press

CHAPTER 5

Comparative and Superlative Adverbs

● **Revise each sentence by writing the correct positive, comparative, or superlative form of the italicized adverb.**

1. The tomcat ran *more faster* than the dog.   _____

2. Tia threw the ball *most farthest* than anyone
   else on the team.   _____

3. My best friend sings *most beautifully* than I do.   _____

4. Josh finished the test *quickly* than Corina.   _____

5. Evan works *most hardest* of anyone.   _____

6. The tiny mouse quivered *less nervous* than it
   did the day before.   _____

7. My teacher gives instructions *most carefully* for
   each assignment.   _____

8. Those two rabbits frolic *playfully* than the others.   _____

9. Of everyone in our speech class, she speaks
   more intelligently.   _____

10. The tired baby cried *loudly* than her twin sister.   _____

11. I arrived at the party *most latest* than my friends.   _____

12. Of all the players on the team, Liz catches *better*.   _____

● **Write two sentences about your day so far. Use a comparative adverb
  in the first sentence and a superlative adverb in the second one.**

13. _____

14. _____

CHAPTER 5

As ... As, So ... As, and *Equally*

● **Write *as*, *so*, or *equally* to complete each sentence.**

1. This dress is not _____ expensive as the ones on that rack.

2. The two students are _____ matched for the competition.

3. The peak of Mt. Whitney isn't nearly _____ high as that of Mt. Everest.

4. I can juggle _____ many balls as the juggler at the fair.

5. She can't read _____ quickly as the rest of the group.

6. The dancers are _____ trained for classical ballet.

7. The amateur musicians played _____ skillfully as the professionals.

8. Today's hike is _____ difficult as yesterday's hike.

● **Write a sentence that includes *as . . . as* or *so . . . as* for each topic.**

9. Your friend tells a funnier joke than you do

_____

10. The championship game was more exciting last year

_____

11. Both the pizza and the spaghetti are spicy

_____

12. Your class collected the same amount of cans for the food drive as you did last year

_____

CHAPTER 5

Fact and Opinion

● **Read each statement. Write *fact* if the statement is a fact or *opinion* if it is an opinion.**

1. Dogs are significantly easier to train than cats. _____

2. Mercury's orbit around the sun is shorter than that of Earth. _____

3. People who eat healthful foods live longer lives. _____

4. Thomas Jefferson signed the Declaration of Independence. _____

5. Our football team won the state championship last year. _____

6. High school athletes do better in school than nonathletes. _____

7. Because of the crowds, summer is the worst time to visit Europe. _____

8. My parents will send me to the college of my choice. _____

9. My mother is a truly talented lawyer. _____

10. You have to receive a law degree in order to practice law. _____

11. Leonardo da Vinci painted *The Last Supper* and the *Mona Lisa*. _____

12. The Renaissance was a time of wonderful art and new ideas. _____

● **Write one fact and one opinion about each topic.**

13. My best friend

Fact: _____

Opinion: _____

14. My favorite song

Fact: _____

Opinion: _____

CHAPTER 5

Adverb Phrases and Clauses

● **Underline the adverb phrases and clauses in the paragraph. Then circle the word each phrase or clause describes.**

Last summer, my family traveled to Italy. Because we had just one week to spend, we planned to visit only three cities. Our first stop was Venice. We took a gondola ride and cruised through the canals. Then we visited St. Mark's Square and gazed in wonder. We walked until our feet were sore. Our next stop was Florence. I could see, as we traveled through the city, many beautiful representations of Florentine art. When I saw Michelangelo's statue of David, I realized what a masterpiece it really was. We could hardly wait to explore Rome, our final stop. Our flight arrived late in the evening. We immediately went to the Trevi Fountain. I threw in a coin so that I could ensure my return someday.

● **Write a short paragraph about a special place you have visited. Include at least four adverb phrases or clauses. Then underline the phrases or clauses and circle the words they describe.**

_____

_____

_____

_____

_____

_____

_____

_____

_____

_____

CHAPTER 5

Single and Multiword Prepositions

● **Circle the two prepositions in each sentence.**

1. The juice from the grapes on the vine was sweet.

2. We put all the pickles into the barrel behind the barn.

3. I saw hundreds of stars through my new telescope.

4. I placed a flower in the vase and tucked one behind my ear.

5. The park near my house features free concerts during the summer.

● **Circle the multiword prepositions in the following sentences.**

6. In spite of the heat we spent the day at the beach.

7. On account of the cloudy skies I couldn't see Saturn.

8. Please back the car out of the garage for me.

9. I decided to concentrate on rain forest insects instead of snakes in my report.

10. Because of the heavy snowfall school closed for the day.

● **Choose the correct preposition to complete each sentence. Write it on the line.**

according to	toward	after	in spite of	between

11. The kittens slept _____ the mother cat and the fireplace.

12. We went out to dinner _____ seeing the movie.

13. The plane began its slow ascent _____ the cloud-filled sky.

14. The baseball game continued _____ the rain.

15. _____ newspaper reports, the hurricane hit at 2:30 a.m.

CHAPTER 5

Evaluating Web Sites

- **Choose the best keyword (or words) to enter into your search engine to research each topic.**

    1. The number of cheetahs living in Africa
       a.African wildlife   c. cheetah population
       b. wildcats   d. cheetahs

    2. The meaning and history of your family's name
       a. name etymology   c. family history
       b. family names   d. names

    3. The last five winners of the Best Picture Oscar at the Academy Awards
       a. best picture   c. Academy Awards statistics
       b. academy awards   d. movie trivia

    4. Important battles that turned the tide in the Civil War
       a. Civil War facts   c. Civil War
       b. great battles   d. Civil War battles

    5. Most recent theories on why dinosaurs became extinct
       a. dinosaur history   c. prehistoric creatures
       b. dinosaur extinction   d. dinosaurs

- **Write the letter of the domain extension you would look for in a URL (web address) to find information on each topic.**

    6. History of the American flag   _____

    7. List of ranks in the Navy   _____   a. *gov*

    8. Jets used by the U.S. Navy   _____   b. *edu*

    9. College class offerings   _____

    10. Registering to vote   _____   c. *mil*

    11. Ford trucks   _____   d. *org*

    12. Postage rates   _____

    13. University campus map   _____   e. *com*

    14. ASPCA animal adoptions   _____

    15. Disneyland's hours of operation _____

CHAPTER 5

Troublesome Prepositions

● **Circle the preposition that correctly completes each sentence.**

1. How did you decide (between   among) red and pink shoes?

2. Taylor was angry (with   at) Elijah for forgetting her birthday.

3. We differ (with   on) the types of clothes we like.

4. Her new kitten looks (like   as if) a tiger.

5. We will choose (between   among) five students for class president.

6. This car differs (with   from) that one in size and speed.

7. Sean is angry (at   with) the idea of being late again.

8. He looked (like   as if) he was going to scream.

9. Carlos differs (with   on) Mom over the college he will attend.

10. Please put the lamp (besides   beside) the chair.

● **Use the prepositions *differ with*, *differ on*, and *differ from* in three sentences. Write about a disagreement with a friend or family member.**

11. _____

12. _____

13. _____

CHAPTER 5

Words Used as Adverbs and Prepositions

● **Write *preposition* or *adverb* to identify how each italicized word is used.**

1. Above us, the jets streaked *across* the sky.   _____

2. The loud noise caused us to look *up*.   _____

3. How many jets swept *over* the throngs of people?   _____

4. The crowd cheered when one jet rolled *over*.   _____

5. We moved *toward* the airplanes to get a better view.   _____

6. Now, I could see everything *around* me.   _____

7. I heard a loud boom as another jet flew *past*.   _____

8. The jet must have flown directly *over*.   _____

9. A loud cheer erupted *from* the people in the crowd.   _____

10. After the show, we all went *inside*.   _____

● **Circle the object of each word in italic type you identified as a preposition. Write the first letter of each word in order on the lines. If your answers are correct, you will reveal the answer to the riddle.**

What sits in a corner while traveling all around the world?

Answer: A ___ ___ ___ ___ ___
                   1   2   3   4   5

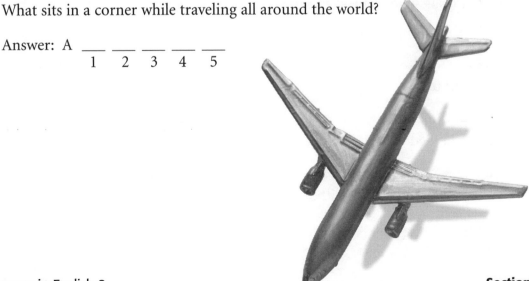

CHAPTER 5

Noun Clauses

● **Rewrite each sentence so that it contains a noun clause. Use the word in parentheses to begin the noun clause. Remember, a noun clause can be a subject, an object, a complement, or an appositive. The first one is done for you.**

1. They couldn't decide on the fair or the museum. (whether)

   They couldn't decide whether they should go to fair or to the museum.

2. I want us to visit New York City this summer, and it is my dream. (that)

   _____

3. The manual explains the construction of the telescope. (how)

   _____

4. I read 10 books over the summer, and that is a fact. (that)

   _____

5. I could see the deer, and I was standing in the meadow. (where)

   _____

6. We didn't know what to make for dinner, so it was up for debate. (what)

   _____

● **Use the following noun clauses in sentences of your own.**

7. that he was the most talented athlete

   _____

8. how to get to the campground

   _____

9. what we needed to know

   _____

10. that the party had started without us

   _____

CHAPTER 5

Prepositional Phrases as Adjectives

● **Underline the adjective phrase in each sentence. Then identify the word it describes by writing it on the line.**

1. Our oceans contain almost countless types of sharks.

2. A shark has many tiny holes on its head that help it find prey.

3. These holes, *ampullae of Lorenzini*, help sharks detect electric signals.

4. The eyes of most sharks are extremely sensitive.

5. The Great White Shark is one of the most well-known species.

6. The lifespan for this shark can reach 100 years.

7. Some books about sharks have frightened people.

8. In fact, most sharks don't want interaction with people.

9. Sharks first appeared eons before the time that today's fish appeared.

10. The time before the dinosaur's period is when sharks first developed.

11. The teeth in a shark's mouth are razor-sharp and tilted inward.

12. Extinction of the giant Megalodon shark occurred approximately 1.6 million years ago.

13. Great White Sharks grow new rows of teeth every one or two weeks.

14. The males of the species are usually smaller than the females.

● **Write the first letter of the boxed words in order on the lines. If your answers are correct, you will reveal the answer to the riddle.**

What occurs once in a minute, twice in a moment, but never in an hour?

Answer: ___ ___ ___   ___ ___ ___ ___ ___ ___ ___   ___

CHAPTER
5

Prepositional Phrases as Adverbs

- **Underline the adverb phrase in each sentence. Then write the word (or words) the adverb phrase describes.**

1. During the Middle Ages many boys wanted to be knights. _____

2. You may wonder about a boy's path to knighthood. _____

3. Usually, a boy started as a page, a knight's assistant. _____

4. A page learned courtly manners early in his training. _____

5. He was loyal to his knight. _____

6. At the age of 14, a page became a squire. _____

7. Squires assisted knights with their horses, spurs, and weapons. _____

8. During this training, a squire worked extremely hard every day. _____

9. After seven years a successful squire was usually knighted. _____

10. To confer knighthood, a nobleman dubbed the squire on the shoulders, using a sword. _____

11. The new knight would always act with bravery and honesty. _____

12. A knight served his king with loyalty for life. _____

- **Sketch a picture showing one scene described above. Write a sentence about your picture, using an adverb phrase.**

_____

_____

5 Prefixes

● **Identify the meaning of the underlined prefix in each group of words. Write the meaning on the line. Refer to the box as needed. You will not use all of the meanings.**

Prefix Meanings

two	not	opposite	to/toward	against	surpassing
too much	back/again	less than	together	bad	many/much
life	before	three	between	one	with

1. <u>il</u>legal, <u>il</u>literate, <u>il</u>logical   _____

2. <u>inter</u>woven, <u>inter</u>connect, <u>inter</u>change   _____

3. <u>bi</u>annual, <u>bi</u>form, <u>bi</u>coastal   _____

4. <u>anti</u>bacterial, <u>anti</u>toxic, <u>anti</u>terrorist   _____

5. <u>multi</u>faceted, <u>multi</u>use, <u>multi</u>media   _____

6. <u>mis</u>take, <u>mis</u>manage, <u>mis</u>inform   _____

7. <u>pre</u>plan, <u>pre</u>nuptual, <u>pre</u>order   _____

8. <u>out</u>pace, <u>out</u>wait, <u>out</u>rank   _____

9. <u>over</u>heated, <u>over</u>wrought, <u>over</u>emotional   _____

10. <u>re</u>match, <u>re</u>iterate, <u>re</u>evaluate   _____

11. <u>mono</u>layer, <u>mono</u>rail, <u>mono</u>culture   _____

12. <u>dis</u>trust, <u>dis</u>allow, <u>dis</u>order   _____

● **Now use the prefixes and meanings above to write a word that matches each definition.**

13. To read again _____

14. To determine before _____

15. Badly spelled _____

CHAPTER

5

Prepositional Phrases as Nouns

● **Underline the noun phrase in each sentence. Write _S_ if the phrase acts as a subject. Write _SC_ if the phrase acts as a subject complement.**

1. Under the tree is my favorite place to read a book.   _____

2. Because of the snow was the reason we had to cancel the play.   _____

3. The spot where we should make our campsite is over this mountain.   _____

4. Beside that meadow was where we saw deer.   _____

5. In front of that trail is the location where we saw the black bear.   _____

6. A bad time to talk on the phone is during a lightning storm.   _____

7. Toward the beach is the direction we should head next.   _____

8. My favorite place to nap was among those wildflowers.   _____

● **Fill in each of the blanks with a prepositional noun phrase.**

1. _____ is where she put the dirty dishes.

2. _____ is my favorite time of day.

3. The reason we rode our bikes is _____.

4. _____ is the best place to watch a baseball game.

5. My normal time for watching TV is _____.

6. _____ is my favorite place to relax.

7. My favorite time to eat pizza is _____.

8. _____ is where we spotted the squirrel.

CHAPTER 5

Self-Assessment

● Check *Always, Sometimes,* or *Never* to respond to each statement.

Writing	Always	Sometimes	Never
I can identify expository writing and its features.			
I can identify facts and opinions.			
I can effectively locate topics on the Internet and evaluate web sites.			
I can identify and use noun clauses.			
I can use prefixes to understand word meanings.			
I include all the key features when I write an expository piece.			

Grammar	Always	Sometimes	Never
I can identify and use different types of adverbs.			
I can identify and use adverbial nouns.			
I can form and use comparative and superlative adverbs.			
I can use *as . . . as, so . . . as,* and *equally.*			
I can identify and use adverb phrases and clauses.			
I can identify and use single and multiword prepositions.			
I can use troublesome prepositions correctly.			
I can identify and use adverbs and prepositions.			
I can identify and use prepositional phrases as adjectives.			
I can identify and use prepositional phrases as adverbs.			
I can identify and use prepositional phrases as nouns.			

● Write the most helpful thing you learned in this chapter.

_____

_____

_____

_____

CHAPTER 6
Kinds of Sentences

● Identify each sentence by writing *declarative, interrogative, imperative,* or *exclamatory.*

1. My best friend gave me a watch for my birthday.   _____

2. Did Andrea remember to walk the dog?   _____

3. Please help with the chores this weekend.   _____

4. That was an incredible game!   _____

5. The grainy sand felt warm between my toes.   _____

6. Is Noah a good tennis player?   _____

7. What an amazing adventure you had!   _____

8. Come with me to play tennis this afternoon.   _____

● Draw a line between each complete subject and complete predicate. Underline the simple subject once and circle the simple predicate.

9. All kinds of animals are trained to perform tricks.

10. Brandon's talented dog does a lot of funny tricks.

11. Prentiss can catch balls in the air.

12. Trained horses jump fences as part of a competition.

13. My friend's Persian cat fetches pom-poms on command.

14. Many people watch killer whales and dolphins in shows at amusement parks.

15. The amazing dolphin might be one of the smartest animals on earth.

Adjective and Adverb Phrases

● Underline the adjective or adverb phrase in each sentence. On the first line, write **PREP** for *prepositional*, **PART** for *participial*, or **INF** for *infinitive*. On the second line, write **ADV** for *adverb* or **ADJ** for *adjective*.

1. These signs are part of a special pet adoption program.

_____ _____

2. The shelter's special pet adoption program began in 2000.

_____ _____

3. Many people donate their time to help the shelter staff.

_____ _____

4. Gaining local popularity, the shelter receives many donations.

_____ _____

5. Many animals in the shelter need immediate medical care.

_____ _____

6. There is never money enough to pay for needed services.

_____ _____

7. Veterinarians volunteer to treat sick and hurt animals.

_____ _____

8. Expanding its services, the shelter recently began taking reptiles.

_____ _____

9. The shelter is a good place to bring kittens and puppies.

_____ _____

10. Every animal eventually is placed in a good home.

_____ _____

11. The best program is the one with free spaying and neutering.

_____ _____

12. Every animal there is treated with love and care.

_____ _____

CHAPTER
6

What Makes Good Persuasive Writing?

● **Read this essay. Then answer the questions.**

> The Bengal tiger is disappearing at an alarming rate. Like other species that have been brought back from near extinction, this animal must be saved.
>
> It is estimated that there are fewer than 3,000 Bengal tigers left in the wild! There are several reasons for this. The primary reason is that tigers are heavily hunted for sport, even though it is outlawed.
>
> Also, an increase in human population and farming has caused the tiger to lose large areas of natural habitat. In India, a government program called Project Tiger was established more than 30 years ago. It now has 23 sanctuaries established for tigers. Even though this wonderful program has made great contributions to saving the tiger, it cannot solve the overall problem.
>
> The human population continues to grow, and the tigers continue to disappear. It is imperative that we protect these beautiful animals.

1. What is the author's position statement?

   _____

2. List two facts that support the author's position.

   _____

   _____

3. List two opinions that support the author's position.

   _____

   _____

● **Choose a position statement from below. Then set up your ideas in a problem/solution chart that you write on a separate sheet of paper. For an example problem/solution chart, see page 140.**

- Our school should have a shorter school day.
- Students should choose their own lunch menus.
- All students should join a sports team or club.
- I should be student body president.

CHAPTER

6 Adjective Clauses

● **Write the adjective clause from the box that best completes each sentence. Underline the noun or pronoun each clause describes.**

where he works as a chef	where people surf	that I read about
whose team won the game	which is my best subject	that I drove
where people camp	who taught me to cook	who loves to dance
which is in Montana	where her horse is kept	that I like best
whom we chose for president	that we'll take soon	that we found

1. Forests _____ should be left free of trash.

2. The car _____ was candy-apple red.

3. My sister, _____ , has a recital tonight.

4. This is the coach _____ .

5. Tyler was the student _____ .

6. Michael showed us the restaurant _____ .

7. Ms. Gomez told us about the test, _____ .

8. The mountain, _____ , is difficult to climb.

9. Maya visited the stables _____ .

10. My grandma is the one _____ .

11. California and Hawaii are two places _____ .

12. Math, _____ , is hard for some people.

13. Summer is the season _____ .

14. The tigers _____ are in danger of extinction.

15. The stray cats _____ all need good homes.

● **Now go back and circle the relative pronouns and subordinate conjunctions.**

CHAPTER 6
Restrictive and Nonrestrictive Clauses

- **Underline the adjective clause in each sentence. Identify it as** *restrictive* **or** *nonrestrictive* **by writing** *R* **or** *NR* **on the line.**

1. Devon, who is a good athlete, made the football team. _____

2. The oranges that you picked are in that basket. _____

3. Neena, who is new this year, went out for the tennis team. _____

4. The kite that stuck in our tree is tangled in the leaves. _____

5. The eggs that dropped on the floor made a mess. _____

6. Yosemite, which is a large national park, is a favorite vacation spot. _____

7. Thanksgiving, which falls on a Thursday, is an American holiday. _____

8. Throw away the umbrella that won't open properly. _____

9. Several restaurants that she suggested sounded good. _____

10. The king, who had won the battle, finally returned home. _____

11. The earrings that I bought are for my mom. _____

12. Yellow, which is my favorite color, brightens up a room. _____

- **Circle the first letter of the noun described by each adjective phrase. Write the letters in order on the lines below. If your answers are correct, you will reveal the answer to the riddle.**

Name two keys that don't unlock doors.

Answer: ___ ___ ___ ___ ___ ___ and ___ ___ ___ ___ ___ ___
          1 2 3 4 5 6   7 8 9 10 11 12

CHAPTER

6 Voice and Audience

• **Choose a word from the box to describe the voice and mood of each paragraph. Then list two phrases or sentences from the paragraph that set the tone.**

| angry | hopeful | enthusiastic | caring | concerned | funny |

Only $2,000 to go! Seaside Animal Shelter is holding a fund-raiser this weekend to raise money for our homeless and sick animals. We know, with your help, that we can do it! Come and join us for the bake sale, raffle, and games. With your participation, we will find each and every animal a loving home!

_____

_____

Our local government has decided to cut down the oak tree in Billows Park. We cannot let this happen! This tree has withstood the test of time. It has been a cherished symbol of our community for more than 200 years! Worst of all, the developer plans to build a huge, ugly condo complex at this site. Don't let the heart of this town be removed!

_____

_____

Mission Hospital has suddenly run short of its blood supply. We, the medical staff of Mission Hospital, implore everyone who is able to donate blood to do so at this weekend's blood drive. We should all be worried about this shortage. It's essential that we build up our reserve supply as soon as possible. This affects all of us. Please help us give you the best care possible.

_____

_____

• **Rewrite the first paragraph so that it conveys a concerned voice and mood. Remember to choose vivid verbs, adjectives, and adverbs that will effectively convey the message to the reader.**

CHAPTER 6

Adverb Clauses

- **Underline the adverb clause in each sentence. Circle each subordinate conjunction.**

1. Because Jim was embarrassed, his face turned red.

2. After the game ended, we drove home.

3. I didn't know what to do when I missed the bus to school.

4. She will make the varsity team if she does well at the tryouts.

5. While Derek washed the car, Carla mowed the lawn.

6. The children acted as if they could stay awake all night.

7. We finished our homework before we went to the movie.

8. Although the water was cold, we enjoyed swimming in the river.

9. I will order the pizza as soon as the guests arrive.

10. The class cheered when Mr. Sanders postponed the test.

- **Write an adverb clause to complete each sentence.**

11. Although _____ ,
    she still felt nervous during her performance.

12. When _____ ,
    I walked on the beach and went scuba diving.

13. You can improve your grades if _____

    _____ .

14. Mom sliced the turkey while Dad _____

    _____ .

CHAPTER 6

Noun Clauses as Subjects

● **Underline the noun clause used as a subject in each sentence. Circle the word that introduces each clause.**

1. That Tia was the best singer in the group was not in question.

2. Whatever everyone decides to do is fine with me.

3. Whether I can afford the trip tops my list of concerns.

4. That we were so excited about the party caused my mother to smile.

5. Whoever baked these cupcakes deserves a blue ribbon!

6. How Tham finally won the race would make a wonderful story.

7. Whomever the coach decides to cut will be disappointed.

8. That we forgot to bring a gift caused us great embarrassment.

● **Write a noun clause used as a subject to complete each sentence.**

9. _____
   may be considered my greatest talent.

10. _____
    was obvious.

11. _____
    has always fascinated me.

12. _____
    is a good idea.

© Loyola Press

CHAPTER

6 Advertisements

- **Identify the propaganda device used in each statement. Then use the same device to write a persuasive statement about the product named.**

| bandwagon | loaded words | testimonial | vague or sweeping generalities |

1. Quarterback Jason Cooper claims, "Sore No More soothes all my aches and pains after a game!"

   _____

   Shampoo: _____

2. Give these cuddly, homeless kittens a safe, warm place to sleep at night.

   _____

   Zoo fundraiser: _____

3. No other store in the city can give you a better deal on a washing machine!

   _____

   Car dealership: _____

4. Even actress Shania Stone uses White 'n' Bright whitening toothpaste!

   _____

   Sports drink: _____

5. Everyone who's anyone loves Shakespeare in the Park!

   _____

   Movie: _____

6. Jake's BBQ makes the spiciest baby back ribs in town!

   _____

   Summer carnival: _____

© Loyola Press

Noun Clauses as Subject Complements

CHAPTER 6

- **Underline the noun clause used as a subject complement in each sentence. Circle the subject.**

1. The best solution is that everyone brings food to share.

2. The main problem was that Jack decided to give up painting.

3. The reason remained that Jack wanted to study art in Europe.

4. The best activity might be when we all go swimming in the ocean.

5. My only worry is that you stay out too late without calling.

6. Yoga is what my sister studies at the recreation center.

7. The question now was who would take over after Jeffrey left.

8. My favorite hour is when the class goes outside to play softball.

9. The fact remains that Galileo improved a telescope developed by someone else.

10. Shane's idea is that we take our vacation in New Zealand.

11. Mom's favorite vacation was when Dad took her to Venice, Italy.

12. The best team member is whoever shows the most spirit.

- **Now go back and circle the first letter of the subject in each even-numbered sentence. Write the letters in order on the lines below. If your answers are correct, you will reveal the answer to the riddle.**

What is the best thing to do if a bull charges you?

Answer: ___ ___ ___ ___ ___ ___ !

CHAPTER 6

Noun Clauses as Appositives

- **Underline the noun clause used as an appositive in each sentence. Circle the noun each clause renames.**

1. The theme that hatred leads to tragedy is central to the play *Romeo and Juliet*.

2. The tradition that Romeo's and Juliet's families must fight does not keep the teenagers apart.

3. Romeo, however, maintains the belief that love will conquer all.

4. Juliet must hide the fact that she and Romeo were married in secret.

5. The friar has the knowledge that the marriage might be dangerous.

6. Juliet appears to be dead, so the truth that she took a sleeping potion isn't known immediately.

7. Unfortunately, Romeo believes the rumor that Juliet has died.

8. The tragedy that Romeo and Juliet both die at the end brings the families together.

- **Find the nouns you circled in the word search. Words can go across, down, or diagonally.**

```
T  O  T  R  I  P  B  M  A  F
R  N  L  H  C  W  E  H  B  A
U  U  S  D  E  T  L  U  N  C
T  H  M  U  A  M  I  K  Y  T
H  K  N  O  W  L  E  D  G  E
C  I  R  E  R  S  F  I  C  T
T  R  A  D  I  T  I  O  N  L
W  E  T  R  A  G  E  D  Y  S
```

CHAPTER 6

Transition Words

● **Circle the transition word or phrase that correctly completes each sentence.**

1. Justin gave his speech to the audience, (while   in addition) Tera waited behind the curtain.

2. Katie held up the advertising sign (in front of   therefore) the new farmer's market.

3. All of us will make it to the game (but   unless) it starts to snow again.

4. Jennifer wouldn't enter her painting in the show (furthermore   because) she felt it wasn't good enough.

5. (However   Unlike), the books will continue to be on sale until Thursday.

6. Jamie wants to go to summer camp; (to begin with   on the other hand), he has an offer for a great part-time job.

7. The Strawberry Festival is lots of fun; (furthermore   therefore), it has the biggest Ferris wheel in the state.

8. (In addition   Before), the hospital needs more volunteers to help with patient care.

9. Bailey stored the boxes in the attic (unless   behind) Grandpa's big trunk.

10. Tyler practiced all summer long, (yet   while) he still didn't make the basketball team.

● **Use each transition word or phrase in a sentence.**

11. (consequently) _____

12. (however) _____

13. (as a result) _____

14. (namely) _____

CHAPTER 6

Noun Clauses as Direct Objects

● Underline the direct object in each sentence. Identify it as a *noun* or a *noun clause* by writing *N* or *NC*.

1. Keisha realized that she should have studied harder for the test. _____

2. Most people take a camera when they go on vacation. _____

3. We decided that we would wait until noon to go to the beach. _____

4. Ian asked Bianca for help in making the spaghetti dinner. _____

5. Mateo wondered how he could go out for two sports. _____

6. My family discussed how we would spend summer vacation. _____

7. I'll choose whatever looks best on me. _____

8. Justin suggested the idea of painting the room green. _____

9. Mom suggested that we help her plant a vegetable garden. _____

10. I wanted flowers rather than vegetables in the garden. _____

11. Many people claimed that they did not enjoy the movie. _____

12. I prefer movies that are funny or about historical figures. _____

13. Penny will perform whichever is the best song for the show. _____

14. Chelsea invited whoever wanted to go to the party. _____

CHAPTER 6

Noun Clauses as Objects of Prepositions

- **Underline the noun clause used as an object of a preposition in each sentence. Then circle the preposition that introduces each clause.**

    1. My friends talked about what were the most violent kinds of storms.

    2. Jake told us about what is known as the F-5 tornado.

    3. A tornado's power is ranked by whatever its wind speed is.

    4. The F-5 is a tornado with what are considered devastating winds.

    5. Most tornadoes occur in what is known as the Midwest's Tornado Alley.

    6. In this area people learn about how they can survive these storms.

    7. People tell frightening stories about what they've seen during the storms.

    8. Warm, moist air is driven east by what has developed into a cold front behind it.

- **Write a few sentences about a strange weather phenomenon you have experienced or read about. Include at least three noun clauses used as objects of prepositions in your writing.**

_____

_____

_____

_____

_____

_____

_____

CHAPTER

6 Suffixes

● **Add a suffix to each italicized word to create a new word that correctly completes the sentence. Write the new word on the line.**

1. Some people want to *legal* a faster speed limit.   _____

2. It is my *responsible* to take out the trash every night.   _____

3. After winning the writing contest, Maya felt *joy*.   _____

4. Our class collected canned foods to donate to a *home* shelter.   _____

5. Our teacher will *specific* which topics we need to study.   _____

6. My sister, Sara, wants to be a *paint* when she grows up.   _____

7. You will need to *active* the alarm before you leave.   _____

8. Cathy uses conditioner to *soft* her long, curly hair.   _____

9. Please ask Jake for some *assist* with these heavy boxes.   _____

10. Jordan dropped *tired* onto the grass after the hike.   _____

11. The judge tried to settle their *disagree*.   _____

12. It was *thought* of him to show up late without calling.   _____

● **Look at the sample word analysis chart on page 138. Copy a blank chart on a separate sheet of paper. Complete the chart for the base word *help* to show how it changes with different suffixes. Use the suffixes *-less*, *-ful*, and *-er*.**

CHAPTER 6

Simple, Compound, and Complex Sentences

● **Write *simple*, *compound*, or *complex* on the lines below to identify each sentence type.**

(1) Have you ever wondered about the formation of a rainbow? (2) It is actually quite simple. (3) When the conditions are right, sunlight passes through drops of water in the air. (4) Sunlight bends while passing through each drop, and the light separates into seven distinct colors. (5) If you want to see a rainbow, the sun must be behind you. (6) The water source must be in front of you. (7) The water source itself is not important; however, you will usually see rainbows after the rain. (8) You can see rainbows year-round, but you will see fewer of them during the winter. (9) Water drops in the air freeze more often in cold weather, and ice scatters light rather than bending it.

1. _____   6. _____

2. _____   7. _____

3. _____   8. _____

4. _____   9. _____

5. _____

● **Use a simple, a compound, and a complex sentence to describe your favorite food, sport, friend, teacher, relative, or school subject.**

Simple: _____

_____

Compound: _____

_____

Complex: _____

_____

CHAPTER

6

Self-Assessment

● Check *Always*, *Sometimes*, or *Never* to respond to each statement.

Writing	Always	Sometimes	Never
I can identify the features of persuasive writing.			
I can identify and write for voice, mood, and audience.			
I can identify advertising and know how to write it.			
I can identify and use transition words.			
I can identify suffixes and use them to understand the meaning of a word.			
I include all the key features when I write a persuasive essay.			

Grammar	Always	Sometimes	Never
I can identify and use declarative, interrogative, imperative, and exclamatory sentences.			
I can identify and use adjective and adverb phrases.			
I can identify and use adjective clauses.			
I can identify and use restrictive and nonrestrictive clauses.			
I can identify and use adverb clauses.			
I can identify and use noun clauses as subjects.			
I can identify and use noun clauses as subject complements.			
I can identify and use noun clauses as appositives.			
I can identify and use noun clauses as direct objects.			
I can identify and use noun clauses as objects of prepositions.			
I can identify and use simple, compound, and complex sentences.			

● Write the most helpful thing you learned in this chapter.

_____

_____

CHAPTER 7

Coordinating Conjunctions

- Circle the correct coordinating conjunction to complete each sentence. Then identify what the conjunction joins by writing words, phrases, or clauses.

1. Bailey couldn't decide between pizza (and   or) spaghetti.   _____

2. I tried to hear the speech, (but   nor) the crowd was too noisy.   _____

3. Cameron double-majored in English (or   and) in biology.   _____

4. Should I take a plane (for   or) a train to get to Chicago?   _____

5. The theater was crowded, (or   yet) I could still see everything.   _____

6. We took the long (for   but) beautiful trail to the mountaintop.   _____

7. Jenna planned to ski (and   but) to get some rest.   _____

8. We will not travel to Spain, (and   nor) will we go to Italy.   _____

9. We can paint the room baby blue (so   or) lemon yellow.   _____

10. It is raining outside, (so   for) we won't go to the beach.   _____

11. We can't get into the museum today, (but   so) we can return tomorrow.   _____

12. Kayla couldn't find her cat, (but   nor) did she have any idea where it might have gone.   _____

- Write two sentences using coordinating conjunctions. Then circle each conjunction and identify what it joins by writing *words*, *phrases*, or *clauses*.

13. _____

    _____   _____

14. _____

    _____   _____

CHAPTER 7

Correlative Conjunctions

- **Circle the correlative conjunctions in each sentence. If the sentence does not have correlative conjunctions, write *none* after the sentence.**

1. Jason is buying not only the baseballs but also the bats and mitts.

2. Either Mindy or Mom will make the cake.

3. Would you like to play games or to go swimming?

4. Neither Lisa nor Eric can make it to class on time.

5. Whether a puppy or a kitten, Annie wants a pet.

6. Lexi and her sister are both making cookies for the party.

7. Both Michael and I will run in the marathon on Saturday.

8. Bianca not only acted in the play but also sang.

9. In case I am late, we can meet at either the restaurant or the museum.

10. Terrance will drive neither the truck nor the van.

11. Let's bring corn and chicken to the neighborhood picnic.

12. Whether Shana will play the leading role or be the director's assistant is still undecided.

- **Write two sentences about school. Include correlative conjunctions in each sentence and circle them.**

13. _____

_____

14. _____

_____

© Loyola Press

CHAPTER 7

What Makes Good Playwriting?

● **Read this excerpt from a play. Then answer the questions below.**

HANNAH: *(straggling behind the others)* This is crazy, you guys. It's a myth, a legend.

MATT: *(turning to face Hannah)* Then why are you here? You have doubted this story all along and yet here you are, right beside us.

ANDY: *(kneels between the rock and boulder)* I think it's here. Look. *(unfolds a tattered piece of paper for friends to examine)*

TERRI: The map shows a tree and a rock just like this!

HANNAH: Oh, sure. This is the only rock and tree around here.

MATT: Just ignore her. Let's see if our detective work has paid off.

(Hannah retreats to downstage right where she busies herself plucking grass. The other three children begin digging. There is a metallic clink as one of the children's shovels makes contact with an object. The three children kneel beside the hole.)

ANDY: *(awestruck)* Wow!

(Hannah gets to her feet and peers at the others from a distance.)

TERRI: Well, we never expected that, did we?

MATT: Hannah, of all of us, you really need to see this!

1. What is most likely the setting for this play? What details lead to that conclusion?

   _____

   _____

2. Would this scene most likely occur in the beginning, middle, or end of the play? Explain your answer.

   _____

   _____

3. Consider Hannah. What do you know about this character based on the details provided in the script?

   _____

   _____

© Loyola Press

CHAPTER 7

Conjunctive Adverbs

● **Circle the conjunctive adverb or parenthetical expression that correctly completes each sentence.**

1. There is only one cookie left; (however   besides), Mom is making more.

2. Dad is firing up the barbecue; (therefore   finally), we should buy some steaks.

3. Pizza is a spicy, delicious food; (later   moreover), it's pretty good for you!

4. I didn't plant enough peas; (then   in fact), I didn't plant enough beans either.

5. The horse is not fully trained; (however   consequently), it's not ready for the show.

6. Jackson built an extra bedroom; (later   still), it became his home office.

7. Luke must paint the playhouse soon; (finally   otherwise), the children will be too big to play in it.

8. Min chose a college close to home; (thus   besides), she'll be home on weekends.

9. Finals were finished today; (besides   finally), summer has arrived!

10. Our house is in the mountains; (indeed   thus), it sits on a peak over 5,000 feet above sea level.

11. Fashion is very important to Kate; (nonetheless   likewise), it is the main interest of her twin sister.

12. The county fair has great food; (furthermore   still), it provides wonderful entertainment.

13. Kaley would like to join the tennis team; (on the other hand   therefore), she is an outstanding volleyball player.

14. The lake is too deep for swimming; (nevertheless   besides), it's too cold outside.

CHAPTER 7

Subordinate Conjunctions

- **Circle each subordinate conjunction and underline the dependent clauses. Not every sentence has a subordinate conjunction.**

   Jackie Robinson was the first African American to play in the American professional baseball leagues. Before that time African Americans played in the Negro Leagues. When Robinson signed his contract with the Brooklyn Dodgers in 1945, he broke the "color barrier." As long as this barrier existed, sports would continue to have teams based on color. Robinson rose to the challenge. Although he dealt with racism on a daily basis, Robinson showed great courage and persistence. He proved to everyone that he belonged in the majors. In 1946 and 1947 Robinson won the National League batting title. He triumphed again in 1949, when he was named the league's most valuable player. Robinson set many team and league records as he played out his career with the Dodgers.

- **Write a few sentences about a favorite sports hero or other famous person. Use at least three subordinate conjunctions in your writing.**

_____

_____

_____

_____

_____

_____

_____

CHAPTER 7

Play Structure and Format

● Read this excerpt from a short story. Use what you know about play structure and format to rewrite this excerpt as part of a script. Be creative as you develop the setting and character descriptions. Use underlining instead of italics to designate stage directions and other details that are not spoken.

Sarah Jane sighed as she watched the sun set beyond the hills. She turned from the doorway, lit the kerosene lamp on the table, and sat down, adjusting her long skirts about her. At last, Sarah Jane spoke. "Why are you here, Mr. Corteney?"

"I've come to inquire about your father's accounts. They are overdue," replied the thin, dour man. He reminded Sarah Jane of an undertaker.

"As I told you before, my father is not here. He is away . . ."

"Seeking his fortune at the silver mines," interrupted Mr. Corteney. "Yes, you told me. But it has been too long, my dear. I cannot extend you credit forever."

Sarah Jane brushed a lock of red hair from her eyes. "I understand, sir. But I can do nothing myself. Father promised he would return by May, in two months' time. Surely waiting two months is better than receiving no money at all."

Mr. Corteney stood up, gathering his hat and cane. "All right," he replied. "I will return, but make no mistake, Miss Sarah Jane. I must be paid at that time, with money or with your farm. The decision will be yours."

He left, slamming the door behind him, and leaving Sarah Jane absorbed in thought.

_____
_____
_____
_____
_____
_____
_____
_____
_____
_____

CHAPTER 7

Troublesome Conjunctions

● **Write the conjunction or the preposition that correctly completes each sentence. Use the words in the box.**

| without | unless | like | as if | as |

1. Justin found it difficult to see the board _____ his glasses.

2. _____ you put on this coat, you will get wet in the rain.

3. Elena looks _____ she has been up all night studying.

4. No one should go outside in the snow _____ boots.

5. That lion looks _____ my cat.

6. We sent a small gift _____ a special thank-you to our coach.

7. Does this candy taste _____ watermelon?

8. _____ an excuse from the doctor, you will be marked absent.

9. Shari ran _____ she were being chased by wild horses.

10. I held on to my hat _____ the wind whipped around me.

11. Please don't walk after dark _____ you have a friend with you.

12. My mom's chocolate cake is _____ no one else's.

13. Jim acted _____ he had won the top prize.

● **Complete each sentence.**

14. I look a lot like _____.

15. I can't go one day without _____.

CHAPTER 7

Interjections

● **Underline the interjection in each sentence. Then write another sentence using the same interjection. You may set it off from the rest of the sentence, or use it as part of an exclamatory sentence.**

1. Oh no, the rain is really pouring down!

_____

2. Ouch! I hit my knee on the corner of the coffee table.

_____

3. Hush! The baby is sleeping.

_____

4. Hooray, they scored another touchdown!

_____

5. No! Don't chew on those slippers.

_____

6. Wow, that show was amazing!

_____

7. Yes, I would love to go ice skating!

_____

8. Hey! Please move your car out of the way.

_____

● **On another sheet of paper, illustrate one of the sentences above to show the emotion the interjection conveys. Put the interjection in a speech bubble.**

CHAPTER 7

Dialog, Monolog, and Asides

● **Read the scene description. Write dialog to develop the scene and characters. Include a monolog and an aside.**

> Sanji is planning a surprise party for her best friend, Rachel, and she is determined to keep it a surprise. Sanji's pesky younger brother, James, however, tricks her into giving up the secret in front of Rachel one rainy afternoon.

_____

_____

_____

_____

_____

_____

_____

_____

_____

_____

_____

_____

_____

_____

_____

_____

_____

_____

_____

_____

Punctuation— Part I

CHAPTER 7

● **Rewrite each sentence, adding or taking out punctuation as necessary.**

1. Mrs Davis asked "How many, students want to go on the field trip?"

_____

2. Shane my little brother was born on, Monday June 7 2004 at lunchtime.

_____

3. Many people love New York New York and I am one of them

_____

4. "Sir you forgot your coat" Tanya told Mr Chang

_____

5. I can't decide whether to visit San Diego California or Dallas Texas

_____

6. Alana Sam and, Trey placed first, second and third, so I heard in the spelling bee

_____

7. "I need" Dad continued "some help with these dishes"

_____

8. His full name which is known only to his friends is Charles S Winslow III

_____

9. Collene the guests are beginning to arrive

_____

10. The children were tired yet they did not want to go to sleep

_____

CHAPTER 7

Punctuation— Part II

● **Rewrite the paragraph, adding or taking out punctuation as necessary.**

Hooray Finally summer had arrived. All year I had been planning a list of things to do go camping with friends, visit my grandparents in Minnesota, repair my bike; and get a part-time job. I couldn't wait to get started however, I didn't know what to do first? Should I visit my grandparents. Should I look for a job! I thought I might work at an animal shelter, namely, Animal Avenue, where my best friend volunteers. I could work early in the morning the rest of the day would be free. Yes. This was going to be the best summer ever.

_____

_____

_____

_____

_____

_____

_____

● **Rewrite the following sentences with the correct punctuation.**

1. We visited several countries namely France Germany and Spain

_____

2. These are the chores I'd like you to do clean your room feed the pets and mow the lawn

_____

3. Wow that game was exciting

_____

4. Did you remember to bring your raincoat

_____

5. Brian carried the boxes upstairs they were very heavy

_____

CHAPTER 7
Idioms, Slang, and Jargon

- **Use an example of idioms, slang, or jargon from the box to complete each line of dialog. Each sentence comes from a different play, so use the context of the dialog within the item to figure out your answer.**

boom swings over the aft deck	lend a hand	in over your head
rubbed him the wrong way	mellow out	ollie that four-set
see eye to eye	sit tight	

1. PERCIVAL: *(disgustedly)* I thought you were my biggest supporter, but now

   I can understand that we no longer ————————————————.

2. MOTHER: *(turns to Dora)* Here, let me ————————————————.
   The task will not be such a chore with both of us doing it.

3. CAPTAIN: *(shouts loudly)* Comin' about. Look alive, mates. Mind your skulls

   as the ————————————————.

4. PROFESSOR: *(pompously)* Are you sure medicine is the right degree for you?
   You failed your midterm exam, and your lab results are less than satisfactory.

   I do believe you are ————————————————.

5. HIPPIE: Hey, ————————————————. Me and my ol' lady see how uptight
   you are, man.

6. LT. NELSON: Men, ———————————————— while I scout over the next bluff.
   Count to 20, then charge over the bluff with everything you've got.

7. BUD: *(in disbelief)* Did you see the way Rudy looked at me? Wow, somehow

   I must have ————————————————.

8. MATT: *(strips off his helmet)* I thought I could ————————————————,
   but I had to bail off board at the last minute.

- **Choose one of the script lines above. With a classmate, write and act out a short dialog that incorporates the line.**

CHAPTER 7

Punctuation—
Part III

- **Rewrite each sentence using quotation marks and italics. Use underlining to indicate italics.**

1. Did you read this article in today's L.A. Times? Dad asked.

   _____

2. Please, my little sister begged, let me go with you to the mall.

   _____

3. The book Renaissance Artists shows a picture of da Vinci's painting The Last Supper.

   _____

4. Have you read the story Lost in Memphis? my teacher asked.

   _____

5. You can find the article Tennis Legends in this month's Sports Illustrated for Kids.

   _____

6. This story, Mr. Loomis said, is based on the poem Among the Leaves.

   _____

7. The lyrics for The Star-Spangled Banner can be found in American Songbook.

   _____

8. Did you see the movie To Touch the Sky: Climbing Mt. Everest last summer?

   _____

9. The Queen Elizabeth 2 is one of the world's largest passenger ships.

   _____

10. Amazing Animal Rescues is my favorite television show! exclaimed Troy.

   _____

CHAPTER 7

Punctuation— Part IV

● **Fill in the circle in front of the answer that shows the correct punctuation.**

1. The Smiths dog
   - ○ The Smith's dog
   - ○ The Smiths dog's
   - ○ The Smiths' dog

2. Words with us and os
   - ○ Words with us' and os'
   - ○ Words with *u*'s and *o*'s
   - ○ Words with *us* and *os*

3. Twenty five years worth
   - ○ Twenty-five year's worth
   - ○ Twenty five years' worth
   - ○ Twenty-five years' worth

4. Sixth graders graduation
   - ○ Sixth-graders graduation
   - ○ Sixth-graders' graduation
   - ○ Sixth grader's graduation

5. Im in the class of 06
   - ○ I'm in the class of '06
   - ○ I'm in the class of 06
   - ○ I'm in the class of "06"

6. My mother in laws purse
   - ○ My mother-in laws' purse
   - ○ My mother's-in-law purse
   - ○ My mother-in-law's purse

7. The forty two cats of the Jones family
   - ○ The Jone's fortytwo cats
   - ○ The Joneses' forty-two cats
   - ○ The Jones' forty-two cats

8. The Unions flag in 63
   - ○ The Unions' flag in "63"
   - ○ The Unions flag in '63
   - ○ The Union's flag in '63

9. Shes a nine year old girl
   - ○ Shes a nine-year-old-girl
   - ○ She's a nine-year-old girl
   - ○ She's a nine year old girl

● **Rewrite each sentence using apostrophes, hyphens, and dashes correctly.**

10. I invited both sisters in law I'm so glad they get along to dinner.

_____

11. Well never forget our high schools ten year reunion.

_____

12. The childrens first aid kit we found it under the sink really came in handy.

_____

CHAPTER 7

Free Verse

● **Write interesting words or phrases that express each abstract word.**

1. exhaustion _____

2. satisfaction _____

3. accomplishment _____

4. tenderness _____

5. joy _____

● **Read the prose passage below. Think about how you could use the information to write a free-verse poem. On a separate sheet of paper, use a word/idea web to brainstorm figurative or sensory language or rhyming words you could use in your poem. For an example of a word/idea web, see page 137. Then write your free-verse poem on the lines below.**

Dew is a deposit of water drops that forms at night when water vapor in the air condenses on the surfaces of objects. Dew forms on clear, still nights. This is because exposed surfaces, such as leaves, blades of grass, and petals lose heat to the atmosphere by radiation at a rate much faster than the surrounding air. These surfaces become cooler than the air and cause any water vapor in the air to condense on the surfaces. The resulting dew appears as tiny beads of water on plant parts.

_____

_____

_____

_____

_____

_____

_____

_____

_____

CHAPTER

7

Capital Letters

● **Rewrite each paragraph using correct capitalization.**

my favorite book is *little house on the prairie* by laura ingalls wilder. while reading the book, I learned a lot about what life was like in america long ago. I was interested to learn how the ingalls family survived on the Prairie. My favorite part was when they met the native americans. I read the book as an english assignment, but now I have read almost the whole Series. i think I will be finished by june, right before Summer.

_____

_____

_____

_____

_____

_____

_____

dr. steinberg is the best veterinarian I know. she graduated from the university of california at davis, the same college uncle troy attended. dr. steinberg treated all of our animals, including my dog happy and my hamster fred. i was very sad when she told me she was moving to tulsa, oklahoma, to be near her family. dr. steinberg will be opening her own practice there called the precious pets clinic.

_____

_____

_____

_____

_____

_____

_____

_____

_____

Self-Assessment

● Check *Always*, *Sometimes*, or *Never* to respond to each statement.

Writing	Always	Sometimes	Never
I can identify the features of playwriting.			
I can identify the structure and format of a play, including character and setting descriptions, dialog, and stage directions.			
I can identify and write dialog, monologs, and asides.			
I can identify and use idioms, slang, and jargon.			
I can identify the features of free verse.			
I include all the key features when I write a scene for a play.			

Grammar	Always	Sometimes	Never
I can identify and use coordinating conjunctions.			
I can identify and use correlative conjunctions.			
I can identify and use conjunctive adverbs.			
I can identify and use subordinate conjunctions.			
I can identify troublesome conjunctions and use them correctly.			
I can identify and use interjections.			
I can identify and use periods and commas.			
I can identify and use semicolons, colons, exclamation points, and question marks.			
I can identify and use quotation marks, italics, and underlining.			
I can identify and use apostrophes, hyphens, and dashes.			
I can identify and use capital letters.			

● What was your favorite part of this chapter? Write an explanation on the lines.

_____

_____

CHAPTER 8

Simple Sentences

● **Diagram the sentences.**

1. Some animals use camouflage.

2. My brother bought me a gold watch.

3. The paintings in the gallery were amazing.

4. My friend in Texas trains on a big chestnut horse.

CHAPTER 8

Appositives

● **Diagram the sentences.**

1. Terrance, my older brother, plays college football.

2. We watched the movie *Sounder* over the weekend.

3. The class read a novel by F. Scott Fitzgerald, an American author.

4. Beverly Cleary, my favorite author, wrote the book *Ramona the Pest*.

CHAPTER 8

What Makes a Good Research Report

- **Read the following paragraph from a research report.
Then answer the questions.**

> Both hurricanes and tornadoes have historically shown themselves to be some of the most dangerous of severe weather phenomena. Consider these two storms: To date, the most destructive tornado on record occurred in 1925—the Tri-State Tornado. It traveled 219 miles, damaging three states in its path—Missouri, Illinois, and Indiana. Three and one-half hours later, 695 people had died and 2,027 were injured. Although technology wasn't available to measure wind speed at the time, today we know that a tornado's winds can reach up to 300 miles per hour. One of the most destructive hurricanes on record occurred in 1992. Hurricane Andrew roared through southern Florida and Louisiana, destroying more than 63,000 homes, causing $20 billion in property damage, and killing 27 people. Just like tornadoes, the destructive force of a hurricane is caused by high winds. Hurricane Andrew was pushed along by winds in excess of 165 miles per hour.

1. What is the author's thesis?

   _____

2. How did the author organize the paragraph?

   _____

3. What two examples does the author use to support the thesis?

   _____

- **Circle the answer that best narrows each topic for a research report.**

   4. Computer games
      a. New technology in computer games
      b. Computer programming
      c. Games around the world

   5. Colleges
      a. Private vs. public colleges
      b. Colleges around the world
      c. The history of colleges

   6. SUVs
      a. SUVs made in the United States
      b. Big cars and trucks
      c. The effects of SUVs on the environment

CHAPTER 8

Compound Sentences

● **Diagram the sentences.**

1. I brought my backpack; however, I forgot my camera.

2. Justin ate four hot dogs; afterwards, he had two pieces of pie.

3. The rain poured down on us, but we finished the baseball game.

4. Shari majored in English; in fact, she has two degrees in modern literature.

CHAPTER 8

Compound
Sentence Elements

● **Diagram the sentences.**

1. Sara and I planted tomatoes in the vegetable garden.

2. Dylan sketched and painted pictures for the art fair.

3. My best friend and I watched movies and played board games.

4. My mother is intelligent and beautiful.

Research and Organization

- **Write notes from this passage on the lines. Each sentence represents a separate note card.**

> France gave the Statue of Liberty to the United States in 1885 as a gift of friendship in recognition of the American Revolution. French sculptor Frederic Auguste Bartholdi was commissioned to design the sculpture. It was supposed to be finished in 1876, for the centennial of the Declaration of Independence. Lack of funds got in the way of a timely completion, however. Lotteries, benefits, auctions, and even prizefights helped raise money for the statue's construction. "Liberty" was finally dedicated on October 28th, 1886, before thousands of spectators.

Note card #1:

_____

_____

Note card #2

_____

_____

Note card #3:

_____

_____

Note card #4

_____

_____

Note card #5:

_____

_____

Note card #6

_____

_____

- **Organize these items into an outline on a separate sheet of paper. Outline main topics, subtopics, and details.**

Sparrow	Cat	Oak	Mammals	Birds	Plants	Trees	Pine
Owl	Animals	Robin	Daisy	Tulip	Whale	Flowers	Horse

CHAPTER 8

Participles

• **Diagram the sentences.**

1. The elephant, reaching with its trunk, took some peanuts.

2. Resting on the beach, Ryan listened to the crashing waves.

3. Grandma entered her pie in the baking contest.

4. My softball team, having won the playoffs, threw a huge celebration party.

CHAPTER
8

Gerunds

● **Diagram the sentences.**

1. Playing tennis is my best skill.

2. My dad enjoys watching old movies.

3. Some dogs are trained for leading the blind.

4. My new hobby, flying kites, is great on a windy spring day.

Citing Sources

CHAPTER 8

● **Write the citation for each source.**

1. Book Title: Seasons in Change
   City and State of Publisher: New York, NY
   Author: Tyler Small, Publication Year: 2002
   Publisher: In Print Publishing

2. Magazine Title: Computer Expert
   Pages of Article: 33–37
   Publication Date: June 8, 2000
   Article Title: Watch Out! New Viruses
   Authors: James Walker, Lin Nguyn

3. Interviewee's Name: Justin Krall
   Date of Interview: May 12, 2004

4. TV Program Title: Mars: The Red Planet
   Date Aired: December 6, 2003
   Network: Explorer Channel
   Network City & State: Dallas, Texas

5. Web Site Name: School Days
   Author: Shane L. Thomas
   Document Title: Making Math Easy
   Web Site Address: www.schooldays.org
   Date Accessed: August 10, 2004

6. Encyclopedia Name: Encyclopaedia Brittanica
   Edition Year: 1999
   Article Title: The American Revolution

7. Newspaper Title: Chicago Journal
   Authors: Cherise Jones, Maggie Wright
   Pages of Article: 3–5
   Publication Date: January 22, 2001
   Article Title: Voting on Election Day

8. Book Title: The General: George Washington
   Publication Year: 1992
   Publisher: WordWorks, Inc.
   Author: Elena Ana Lopez
   City and State of Publisher: Chicago, IL

1. _____
   _____
   _____

2. _____
   _____
   _____

3. _____
   _____

4. _____
   _____
   _____

5. _____
   _____
   _____

6. _____
   _____

7. _____
   _____
   _____

8. _____
   _____
   _____

CHAPTER
8

Infinitives

● **Diagram the sentences.**

1. Jesse asked me to join the club.

2. Our idea, to plan a surprise party, excited the whole family.

3. Her family has a room to rent.

4. We were excited to win first prize.

CHAPTER 8

Adjective Clauses

● **Diagram the sentences.**

1. My bike, which was bright red, is now baby blue.

2. Taylor gave Dad a gift that she bought in China.

3. She is the one whose song was chosen for the school play.

4. Brandon was the player whom they selected for team captain.

© Loyola Press

Reference Tools

● **Identify the research tool you would use to find information about each topic. Some items may have more than one answer.**

| encyclopedia | almanac | bibliographical reference |
| catalog | atlas | *Reader's Guide to Periodical Literature* |

1. The top songs of 1997 _____

2. A book about the legend of King Arthur _____

3. The history of movies in the United States _____

4. The life of Dr. Martin Luther King Jr. _____

5. Annual rainfall numbers for Arizona _____

6. Magazine articles on Italian cooking _____

7. A book about raising Siamese cats _____

8. Mountainous regions in Argentina _____

9. The American Revolution _____

10. The basketball career of Michael Jordan _____

11. Articles on general car maintenance _____

12. The political boundaries of Poland _____

13. Famous scientists of the 20th century _____

14. Pulitzer Prize winners _____

15. Magazine articles on Olympic diving _____

CHAPTER 8 Adverb Clauses

● **Diagram the sentences.**

1. Since Keisha joined our class, discussions are much more interesting.

2. Although Carter loves the rain, he is afraid of thunderstorms.

3. We will show the slides when Lisa returns from her vacation.

4. The nature group hiked up the mountain before the sun went down.

CHAPTER 8 Noun Clauses

● **Diagram the sentences.**

1. That the house needs a good paint job is obvious.

2. How the robbers escaped with the money is still a mystery.

3. The biggest problem was that we could not find the tickets.

4. My English teacher presented a homework pass to whoever read the most books.

CHAPTER 8 Multiple-Meaning Words

● **Look at the underlined word in the first sentence. Circle the sentence below in which the underlined word has the same meaning.**

1. Mia was <u>bound</u> toward home after the party.
   a. Dylan is <u>bound</u> to realize his mistake.
   b. Watch the bunny <u>bound</u> around the backyard.
   c. The passengers on the train were westward <u>bound</u>.

2. Turn on the porch <u>light</u> after dark.
   a. These boxes are <u>light</u> enough to carry upstairs.
   b. The <u>light</u> in the kitchen needs a new bulb.
   c. Terrance will <u>light</u> a fire so we can roast marshmallows.

3. All classes were <u>present</u> for the principal's speech.
   a. What kind of <u>present</u> did you buy for Mom?
   b. I would like to <u>present</u> my sister, Lauren.
   c. Is everyone in the club <u>present</u> today?

4. Do you think that it's <u>right</u> to tell secrets?
   a. Jason knew he was <u>right</u> to return the money he found.
   b. Please turn <u>right</u> at the next corner.
   c. For this exercise, stretch your <u>right</u> arm over your head.

5. Kaitlyn followed the fox's <u>tracks</u> into the woods.
   a. With his computer, Mario <u>tracks</u> all the Web sites he has used.
   b. Kenny left <u>tracks</u> with his boots in the snow.
   c. The train <u>tracks</u> ran from California all the way to Texas.

● **Write two sentences for each word, using it in different ways.**

6. wind

_____

_____

7. pound

_____

_____

8. fair

_____

© Loyola Press

CHAPTER 8

Diagramming Review

● **Diagram the sentences.**

1. Kendra and Luke tried to stop, but their sled crashed into the snow bank.

2. My brother Aaron and his friend climbed Mt. Whitney and hiked the Pacific Coast Trail to Washington.

3. The golden lion, roaring with all its might, rushed at its unsuspecting prey.

4. Dr. Phillips, who treats all my animals, asked me to help with the new pet adoption program.

Self-Assessment

- **Check *Always*, *Sometimes*, or *Never* to respond to each statement.**

Writing	Always	Sometimes	Never
I can identify the features of a research report.			
I can take effective notes and organize an outline.			
I can identify and cite sources.			
I can identify and use reference tools.			
I can identify multiple-meaning words and use them correctly.			
I include all the key features when I write a research report.			

Grammar	Always	Sometimes	Never
I can diagram simple sentences.			
I can diagram sentences with appositives.			
I can diagram compound sentences.			
I can diagram compound elements in sentences.			
I can diagram sentences with participles.			
I can diagram sentences with gerunds.			
I can diagram sentences with infinitives.			
I can diagram sentences with adjective and adverb clauses.			
I can diagram sentences with noun clauses.			

- **Explain how learning to diagram a sentence will help you be a better writer.**

_____

_____

_____

_____

_____

_____

_____

© Loyola Press

Word/Idea Web

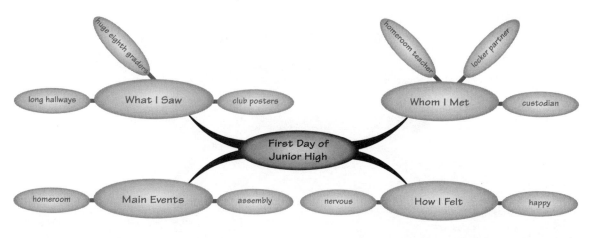

Narrative Map

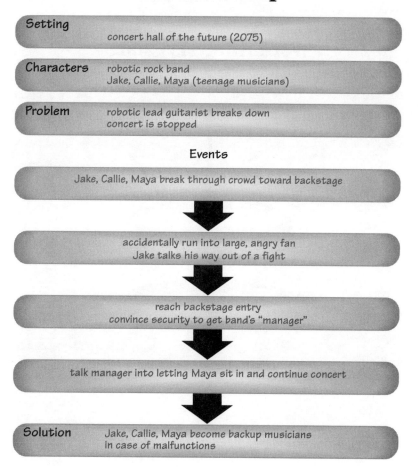

Compare and Contrast Chart

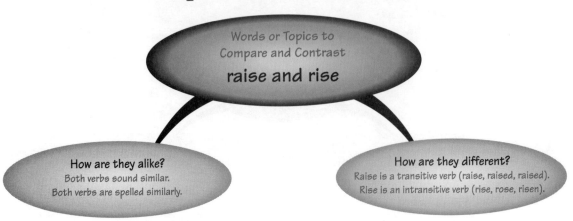

Words or Topics to
Compare and Contrast
raise and rise

How are they alike?
Both verbs sound similar.
Both verbs are spelled similarly.

How are they different?
Raise is a transitive verb (raise, raised, raised).
Rise is an intransitive verb (rise, rose, risen).

Word Analysis Chart

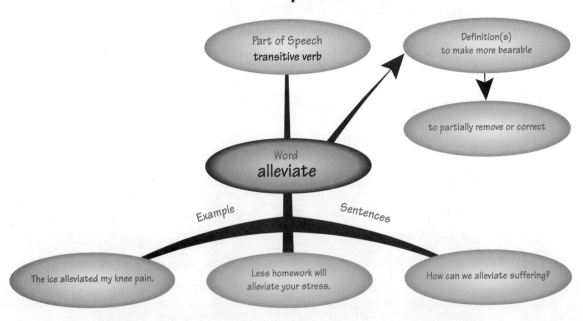

Part of Speech
transitive verb

Definition(s)
to make more bearable

to partially remove or correct

Word
alleviate

Example

Sentences

The ice alleviated my knee pain.

Less homework will
alleviate your stress.

How can we alleviate suffering?

Steps in a Process Chart

Title: Egg Basket Cupcakes

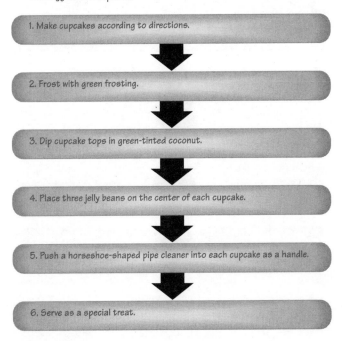

1. Make cupcakes according to directions.

2. Frost with green frosting.

3. Dip cupcake tops in green-tinted coconut.

4. Place three jelly beans on the center of each cupcake.

5. Push a horseshoe-shaped pipe cleaner into each cupcake as a handle.

6. Serve as a special treat.

Paragraph Plan

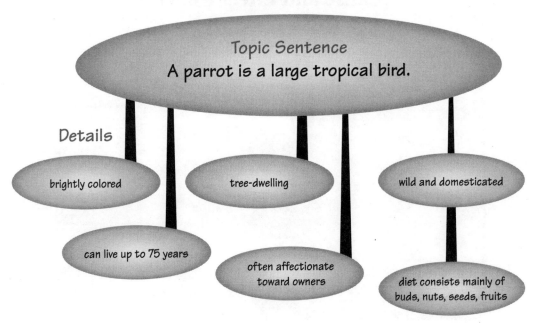

Topic Sentence
A parrot is a large tropical bird.

Details

brightly colored

tree-dwelling

wild and domesticated

can live up to 75 years

often affectionate toward owners

diet consists mainly of buds, nuts, seeds, fruits

Problem and Solution Chart

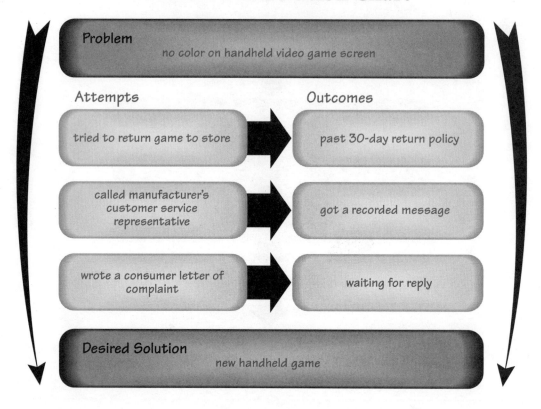

Problem

no color on handheld video game screen

Attempts | Outcomes

tried to return game to store → past 30-day return policy

called manufacturer's customer service representative → got a recorded message

wrote a consumer letter of complaint → waiting for reply

Desired Solution

new handheld game

Cause and Effect Chart

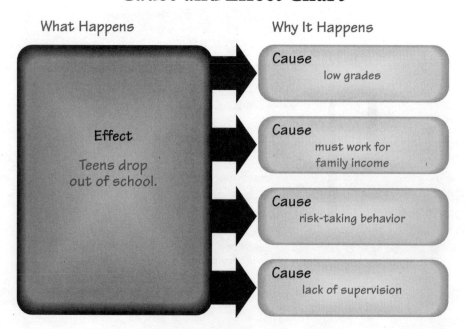

What Happens | Why It Happens

Effect

Teens drop out of school.

Cause low grades

Cause must work for family income

Cause risk-taking behavior

Cause lack of supervision